## ALSO BY ROBERT LOWELL

*Land of Unlikeness* (1944)

*Lord Weary's Castle* (1946)

*The Mills of the Kavanaughs* (1951)

*Life Studies* (1959)

*Phaedra* (translation) (1961)

*Imitations* (1961)

*For the Union Dead* (1964)

*The Old Glory* (plays) (1965)

*Near the Ocean* (1967)

*Prometheus Bound* (translation) (1967)

*The Voyage and Other Versions of Poems by Baudelaire* (1968)

*Notebook 1967–68* (1969; *Notebook*, revised and expanded edition, 1970)

*History* (1973)

*For Lizzie and Harriet* (1973)

*The Dolphin* (1973)

*Selected Poems* (1976; revised edition, 1977)

*Day by Day* (1977)

*The Oresteia of Aeschylus* (translation) (1978)

*Collected Prose* (1987)

*Collected Poems* (2003)

*The Letters of Robert Lowell* (2005)

*Selected Poems: Expanded Edition* (2007)

*Words in Air: The Complete Correspondence Between Elizabeth Bishop and Robert Lowell* (2008)

*New Selected Poems* (2017)

*The Dolphin Letters, 1970–1979: Elizabeth Hardwick, Robert Lowell, and Their Circle* (2019)

# THE DOLPHIN

# THE DOLPHIN

*Two Versions, 1972–1973*

# ROBERT LOWELL

*Edited by Saskia Hamilton*

FARRAR, STRAUS AND GIROUX

NEW YORK

Farrar, Straus and Giroux
120 Broadway, New York 10271

Grateful acknowledgment is made to the Harry Ransom Center at the University of Texas at Austin for permission to reprint scans of the 1972 manuscript of *The Dolphin*.

Library of Congress Control Number: 2019020295
ISBN: 978-0-374-53827-9

Designed by Jonathan D. Lippincott

Our books may be purchased in bulk for promotional, educational, or business use. Please contact your local bookseller or the Macmillan Corporate and Premium Sales Department at 1-800-221-7945, extension 5442, or by e-mail at MacmillanSpecialMarkets@macmillan.com.

www.fsgbooks.com
www.twitter.com/fsgbooks • www.facebook.com/fsgbooks

10  9  8  7  6  5  4  3  2  1

# Contents

## THE DOLPHIN MANUSCRIPT (1972)

# Introduction

> I have learned what I wanted from the mermaid
> and her singeing conjunction of tail and grace.[1]

"One man, two women" is what Robert Lowell called "the common novel plot" of *The Dolphin*. It is a book of love poems, and therefore a book of being driven off course, of doubt and vacillation. The protagonist is a poet (a "suffering hero?"[2] as Lowell ventured in an interview), who, while in England and away from his wife and daughter in New York, falls in love with a woman named Caroline, both a figure in the plot and the actual person, Caroline Blackwood, to whom the book is dedicated. He thinks of his pursuit of Caroline and of his own art as continuous. A sense of impending mortality haunts him, as well as responsibility to and anxiety about children; Caroline's, with whom he now lives; and his daughter, Harriet, in America. But more cutting and urgent is another "rapier voice,"[3] that of his wife, Lizzie (Elizabeth Hardwick), speaking in letters and through the telephone cables. In the course of the story, he falls in love, has a recurrence of mania, suffers hallucinations and hospitalization, recovers, vacillates in an agony of indecision, goes back home to find no true answer, then makes his choice. In the manuscript version, the choice, made at Christmas, is followed the next year by the birth of a son (Robert Sheridan) and "a happiness so slow burning, it is lasting."[4] In the published version, the coming of the child precedes, and helps him to find, his resolution.

The riddles that all poems make and solve helped Lowell survive those days—"it seems our insoluble lives sometimes come clearer in

---

1. *Mermaid* 1:1–2. Cf. Milton: "Th' old Dragon under ground, [. . .] Swindges the scaly Horrour of his foulded tail" ("On the Morning of Christ's Nativity" 168, 172; the poem echoes elsewhere in *The Dolphin*, too). Cf. also T. S. Eliot: "I have heard the mermaids singing, each to each" ("The Love Song of J. Alfred Prufrock" 124).

2. "The Poet Robert Lowell—Seen by Christopher Ricks," *The Listener*, June 21, 1973, p. 831.

3. "On the End of the Phone" 5.

4. "Nine Months" 2 [*Burden* 8], "The Dolphin" manuscript.

writing."[1] While "pursuing my ear that knows not what it says,"[2] Lowell created a series of poems that recount an experience of recovery, survival, guilt, and grief coincident with "beguilement and the storm" of erotic forces. To borrow from Coleridge, it is the choice of sensations[3]— the poet alert to his own feeling and thought alongside the look of London crowds at night, or the sounds of "the crude and homeless wet" of rain against the glass, or the memory of Lizzie's intonations, or the experience of Caroline's "humor and fragility"—that the poems sift. More than writing per se, the writing of this book, the shaping of the drama, is part of the narrative—for Lowell found in the writing of it a form of equipoise, balancing in his mind his exhilaration and desires, his conflicting responsibilities, and his artistic judgment.

As with all of Lowell's deeply allusive work, he invites us to think of his art against the background of tradition. The verse form is an adapted sonnet, consisting mainly of fourteen lines, rhyming internally to no set scheme, with something of a sonnet's thought structure. Among the ideals he invokes is accuracy, which was already on his mind when he was revising poems for *Notebook*, the collection that immediately preceded *The Dolphin*. He wrote to Marianne Moore in January 1970 about a recent poem of hers:

> What startled was your generosity of thought, and the accuracy in carrying it out. I mean that when most people might feel they've\d/ found a good enough figure, you go on to accuracy.[4]

Accuracy meant more than exact description, but figures and represented forms quick with life and various of feeling or thought. He had said

1. Robert Lowell, "After Enjoying Six or Seven Essays on Me," *Salmagundi* (Spring 1977), p. 113; reprinted in Robert Lowell, *Collected Poems*, ed. Frank Bidart and David Gewanter (New York: Farrar, Straus and Giroux, 2003), p. 991.

2. Lowell, "After Enjoying Six or Seven Essays on Me," p. 112; reprinted in Lowell, *Collected Poems*, p. 991.

3. Cf. Coleridge's notebooks, ca. November 1803, Borrowdale: "the *choice* of sensations, I in much pain leaning on my Staff, and viewing the clouds and hearing the Church Bell from Crosthwaite Church"; quoted in Alethea Hayter, *A Voyage in Vain: Coleridge's Journey to Malta in 1804* (London: Faber & Faber, 1973), p. 35. See also Lowell's Coleridge sonnets in *History*, and Helen Vendler's recollection of Lowell's conversation about Coleridge in "Robert Lowell's Last Days and Last Poems," *Robert Lowell: Interviews and Memoirs*, ed. Jeffrey Meyers (Ann Arbor: University of Michigan Press, 1988), p. 310.

4. Robert Lowell to Marianne Moore, January 18, 1970, Marianne Moore Collection, The Rosenbach.

of his most celebrated book, *Life Studies*,[1] that his ambition was for each poem to "seem as open and single-surfaced as a photograph," what Michael Hofmann has described as "an Imagism enriched with psychological notes, with hardheadedness, with implication."[2] But Lowell subsequently came to see the ambition as a limitation, finding it "severe to be confined to rendering appearances." The material of the *Life Studies* poems was largely "recollection," of his childhood and family life. In the *Notebook* sonnets, which led to *The Dolphin*, the mix of the immediate present moment with memory, "the day-to-day with the history"—"always the instant, sometimes changing to the lost"—resulted in poems that are "more jagged and imagined." This is the accuracy he was after, "things I felt or saw, or read" becoming "drift in the whirlpool."[3] He would later "pray," in his poem "Epilogue," "for the grace of accuracy."[4]

Perhaps his decision to be "frank, open and vulnerable"[5]—or "simple, sensuous and passionate," from Milton's definition of poetry[6]—while in the grip of writing his poems creates the special style of *The Dolphin*. In the spring of 1971 Lowell was thinking about "the difficult poetry I grew wise and confused on in the thirties"[7]—William Empson and Hart Crane, he offered as examples, and others inspired not only by sixteenth- and seventeenth-century poetry but by the critics who wrote so discerningly about it. "Now that obscure poetry is perhaps out of fashion, one must pay homage to its supreme invention and exploration."[8] In the summer of 1971,

---

1. Published in 1959.

2. Michael Hofmann, *Where Have You Been? Selected Essays* (New York: Farrar, Straus and Giroux, 2014), p. 72.

3. Ian Hamilton, "A Conversation with Robert Lowell," *the Review*, No. 26 (Summer 1971): 13–14.

4. Lowell, "Epilogue" 16, *Day by Day* (1977).

5. Robert Lowell, review of *The Testing-Tree*, by Stanley Kunitz, *The New York Times Book Review*, March 21, 1971, p. 1.

6. Milton wrote that in contrast to logic, "Poetry would be made subsequent, or indeed rather precedent, as being less suttle and fine, but more simple, sensuous and passionate" (*Of Education* [1644]). Lowell first contended with the turbulence in Milton's definition ("less suttle and fine, but more simple, sensuous and passionate") in a 1940 letter: "I must keep spiritually alive and brilliantly alive, for poetry is, as the moral Milton conceded in practice and precept, a sensuous, passionate, brutal thing" (Robert Lowell to A. Lawrence Lowell, [February 1940], in Robert Lowell, *The Letters of Robert Lowell*, ed. Saskia Hamilton [New York: Farrar, Straus and Giroux, 2005], p. 25).

7. Robert Lowell to Mrs. Adrienne Conrad [Rich], March 29, 1971, in Elizabeth Hardwick and Robert Lowell, *The Dolphin Letters, 1970–1979*, ed. Saskia Hamilton (New York: Farrar, Straus and Giroux, 2019), p. 163.

8. Lowell, review of *The Testing-Tree*, p. 1.

he spoke of Ezra Pound's *Pisan Cantos* as the work of "a hard, angular, in some ways shrill and artificial man" who "by courage let the heart break through his glass ribs."[1] The first sonnets, with their "unnecessarily grand obscurities" that he later tried to "comb out,"[2] arose conditionally from the strange explosive mix of his experience while his old models contended behind the scenes. The result is poetry that is emotionally and tonally various, at times oblique in its leaps of thought and address, in its switching between British and American idioms, humorous and suffering and self-humoring, truth-telling and "sidestepping."[3]

Lowell began writing sonnets about his new love shortly after his affair with Caroline Blackwood began in May 1970. In late June, he telegraphed Hardwick that he would not be returning to New York, and two weeks later he was hospitalized in London for mania. Blackwood departed, and Hardwick, moved by his distress, visited him at the London hospital in early August. She found him in a very weakened state and reported that he could "hardly write, writing a few poems (they're all right)."[4] He was released from the hospital in late August, and by October, he had thirty poems, "the Romantic romance of a married man in a hospital," as he wrote to his friend Elizabeth Bishop.

By the end of November Lowell had "about ninety," composing "at a great rate, even scribbling lines down during a dinner"[5]—more than a poem a day for two months. Among these were several written in the voices of the "two women," based on transposed letters and conversations. (The story of Lowell's use of Hardwick's original letters—their wide-angle portrayal of her feelings, what he wanted from them for his poetry—is told in *The Dolphin Letters, 1970–1979: Elizabeth Hardwick, Robert Lowell, and Their Circle*.) He went home to New York for the Christmas holiday and broke with Hardwick, then returned to

---

1. Ian Hamilton, "A Conversation with Robert Lowell," p. 16. He used the same metaphor when talking about borrowing from the novel form (for *Notebook*), "because I think poetry must escape from its glass" (p. 17).

2. Robert Lowell to Elizabeth Bishop [October 5, 1970] in *The Dolphin Letters*, p. 110.

3. "On the End of the Phone" 1. Cf. "Israel" 1 [*Lines from Israel* 3], *Notebook* (1970).

4. Blair Clark's notes of conversations with Elizabeth Hardwick, Blair Clark's Robert Lowell Collection 1938–1983, Harry Ransom Center, the University of Texas at Austin; see *The Dolphin Letters*, p. xlii.

5. Robert Lowell to Elizabeth Hardwick, November 28, 1970, in *The Dolphin Letters*, p. 135.

England in the new year. Later that winter came the news that Black-wood was pregnant.

Lowell wrote new poems in the spring of 1971, including the first and final sonnets,[1] and found his figure of the dolphin, the tutelary spirit of the book.[2] (The dolphin is a symbol of Apollo, one of the gods of poetry, and of healing and divination; and the word, some scholarship suggests, is etymologically linked to δελφύς or *delfys*, for "womb." As a classicist in college, Lowell would also have known the tale, from Herodotus and Ovid, of the poet Arion, who was rescued from captivity by dolphins.) Even as he continued to add new sonnets written during Caroline's pregnancy, the arc of the plot had been shaped. All the while, Lowell hesitated to plan the publication of the work, sensing that Hardwick "will feel bruised by the intimacy. She should win all hearts but what is that when you are left, and left again in print?"[3] He nevertheless chose to publish a selection of fourteen poems in *the Review* that summer, and wrote what he thought would be the last of the poems at the birth of Sheridan in September.[4]

By the end of 1971 Lowell had assembled a fully shaped manuscript of "about eighty poems."[5] He invited Frank Bidart to England to help finalize this draft, going over the poems, sometimes dictating lines for Bidart or Blackwood to add to the typescript. They finished a version in early 1972, and Bidart brought a photocopy back to America. Copies were given or sent to Bishop, William Alfred, and Stanley Kunitz, among others. Their strong reactions—admiration and shock—caused Lowell to rethink the book.

All three objected to Lowell's use of Hardwick's letters and conversation. Bishop was particularly uneasy with Lowell's revisions of Hardwick's written words (*"art just isn't worth that much,"* she wrote).[6] She was also critical of the plot sequence at the end. She found the shift from his final New York visit (in the *Flight to New York* sequence) to the "change, decision,

---

1. "Fishnet" and "Dolphin."

2. Lowell: "Most artistic transformations are symbols [. . .] The anguish of the most original is its tension and ungainliness in descending to the actual, the riches of days" (review of *The Testing-Tree*, p. 1).

3. Robert Lowell to Stanley Kunitz, April 25, 1971, in *The Dolphin Letters*, p. 173.

4. When Lowell further revised *The Dolphin* in the spring and summer of 1972, he added new poems.

5. Robert Lowell to Frank Bidart, [December 6 or 8? 1971], in *The Dolphin Letters*, p. 225.

6. Elizabeth Bishop to Robert Lowell, March 21, 1972, in *The Dolphin Letters*, p. 259.

or whatever happens" afterward (his return to Caroline, the news of her pregnancy¹) "too sudden—after the prolongation of all the first sections, the agonies of indecision, etc.—(wonderful atmosphere of life's *stalling* ways . . .)." After the end of *Flight to New York*, with its "shadow of departure"² from Lizzie and their life together, "there is no actual return to England—and the word BURDEN and then the question 'Have we got a child?'³ sounds almost a bit Victorian-melodramatic." She thought his character had to get himself "back to England *before* the baby appears like that."

Lowell did not want to lose the voice of the Lizzie character, but he decided to change what he came to see as a "rather callous happy ending"⁴ and to "somehow blunt and angle the letters"⁵ so that they seemed not so much documentary as the recording of arguments in his memory and mind. He described to Bidart the changes he was making:

> Several of the early letters, From my Wife[,] are now cut up into Voices (often using such title) \changing mostly pronouns/ as if I were speaking and paraphrasing or repeating Lizzie.⁶

To Kunitz, he wrote:

> The long birth sequence will come before the Flight to New York, a stronger conclusion, and one oddly softening the effect by giving a reason other than \new/ love for my departure. Most of the letter poems—E. B.'s objection they were part fiction offered as truth—can go back to your old plan, a mixture of my voice, and another voice in my head, part me, part Lizzie, \italicized,/ paraphrased, imperfectly, obsessively heard.⁷

---

1. Indicated in "Knowing," the first sonnet in the subsequent *Burden* sequence in "The Dolphin" manuscript. Cf. OED: "That which is borne in the womb, a child" ("Burden" 4, *Oxford English Dictionary*, Vol. I [1933]).
2. "Christmas 1970" 14 [*Flight to New York* 8 10], "The Dolphin" manuscript.
3. "Knowing" 6 [*Burden* 1], "The Dolphin" manuscript.
4. Robert Lowell to Elizabeth Bishop, Easter Sunday [April 4], 1972, in *The Dolphin Letters*, p. 264.
5. Robert Lowell to Frank Bidart, May 15, 1972, in *The Dolphin Letters*, p. 282.
6. Robert Lowell to Mr. Frank Bidart, April 10, [1972], in *The Dolphin Letters*, p. 272.
7. Robert Lowell to Stanley Kunitz, April 24, 1972, in *The Dolphin Letters*, p. 276.

The alternative plots—one closely aligned with the true unfolding of events, the other fictive—did not alter the truth of what Lowell saw (by the spring of 1972) as a consequence somehow fated.[1] He felt that the sequence of poems about going home to face his wife and daughter (*Flight to New York*) "is the real, though not chronological ending" and "the real truth of the story."[2]

Even so, the change alters the key in which we hear those poems, written in the uncertainty of the moment, revised and narratively placed after Lowell had lived with the outcome of his decision. He had composed *Flight to New York* in November and December 1970, before and during the Christmas visit to his wife and daughter. In November, he was still wavering, but believed that he would be returning to them for good. He had asked Hardwick to take him back, and wrote to her on November 16:

> I have been pouring out poems, and almost have a little book, in the same form as *Notebook*, but much smaller. I've even anticipated my landing in New York. You see I am back home.[3]

On November 30, he wrote to her again:

> I still do nothing much but bury my indecisions in many many poems. I think I have ninety now and a tall house of draft and discard. I am very bad company because I am so removed. You won't enjoy me. However I am coming to see you and dear Harriet, not Blair. So you'll hear from me at once.[4]

But by mid-December, he had changed his mind again. He wrote to Kunitz on December 12:

---

1. Compare the final *Notebook* poem, "Obit," a love poem to Hardwick, with the version in *For Lizzie and Harriet*, a new first line underscoring what he had come to feel by 1972: "Our love will not come back on fortune's wheel—"
2. Robert Lowell to Frank Bidart, May 15, 1972, in *The Dolphin Letters*, p. 282.
3. Robert Lowell to Mrs. Robert Lowell [Elizabeth Hardwick], November 16, 1970, in *The Dolphin Letters*, p. 132.
4. Robert Lowell to Mrs. Robert Lowell [Elizabeth Hardwick], November 30, 1970, in *The Dolphin Letters*, p. 136.

Nothing is settled forever, but I imagine Lizzie and I are breaking. I pray it may be no more cruel than it has to be, and a little less. It's all been rather killing, for months now not manic but cold, sober, & anxious sober.[1]

Lowell wrote to Bishop too of his change of heart as his trip neared:

I'll be in New York staying with Blair Clark about the time you get this. I think Lizzie and I are going to break. I should have done it much more cleanly some time ago. But I can't. I wonder if anyone in his right mind could. I am back to see Lizzie and Harriet, things are not even now quite settled, but they must be.[2]

Bishop later wondered if "flight" in the title *Flight to New York* "is the right word here? (even if you do fly)."[3] A reader of *The Dolphin* might feel invited to think of another kind of flight, but is then disinvited by the very outcome of the story.[4]

## TWO VERSIONS

There is no comfortable category for Lowell's sonnets—the work of six years that resulted in the publication of five volumes of poetry,[5] which he revised again in subsequent reprintings[6]—nor can a "stable text" be presented. While there is nothing remarkable about a writer amending his or her work, Lowell's practice of it was unusually public. As he reported, "I couldn't stop writing, and have handled my published book as

1. Robert Lowell to Stanley Kunitz, December 12, 1970, box 63, folder 6, Stanley Kunitz Papers, 1900–2014 (mostly 1960–2005), Manuscripts Division, Department of Rare Books and Special Collections, Princeton University Library.
2. Robert Lowell to Elizabeth Bishop, [December 1970], in *The Dolphin Letters*, p. 139.
3. Elizabeth Bishop to Robert Lowell, March 21, 1972, in *The Dolphin Letters*, pp. 258–59.
4. Cf. William Empson's two senses of flight (taking wing, fleeing) in his poem "Aubade."
5. *Notebook 1967–68* (1969) was published twice in a first and a revised printing. *Notebook* (1970) was a substantial revision of *Notebook 1967–68*. The poems in *Notebook* were further revised and rearranged, then published in two separate volumes, *For Lizzie and Harriet* (1973) and *History* (1973). *The Dolphin* (1973) was a new book of poems.
6. See Lowell, *Collected Poems*, pp. 1074, 1127, and 1131.

if it were manuscript."[1] "Endless days revising our revisions" were spent, from handwritten first drafts to typed manuscripts, magazine publications, and typeset book galleys, and going past these to paperback editions and further changes in Jonathan Raban's *Robert Lowell's Poems: A Selection* (1974), Lowell's own *Selected Poems* (1976), and his revised *Selected Poems* (1977), as well as lists of further corrections that he left with his friends[2] or may have written in their copies of his books. The printed page allowed him to notice things he had overlooked in manuscript and wanted to put right.

The closest metaphor for Lowell's freedom with the printed record, one critic suggests, is to the fluidity of song in performance[3]—a freedom tolerated by his publishers in America and Great Britain, who bore the cost of producing books that had simultaneously circulating versions of the same poems, and that as stock and backlist did not have the same temporally brief life as a song played for an audience.[4] Like Erasmus before him, who had hoped that the reader of new editions of the *Adagia* will "have gained twice, not lost twice,"[5] Lowell also hoped that "there has been increase of beauty, wisdom, tragedy, and all the blessings of this consuming chance."[6] But what it asks of a reader did trouble him, and in some moods he thought despairingly of those who might "spend lifetimes listing and living variants";[7] or of the "still target" he held up "for the critic who knows that most second thoughts, when visible, are worse thoughts."[8] (Tennyson asked in his poem "Sea Dreams," "Is it so true that second thoughts are best? | Not first, and third, which are a riper first?") Any further thoughts after the first, second, and third that Lowell left behind are final in authority only because of his death.

1. Robert Lowell, "A Note to the New Edition," *Notebook* (1970), p. 264.

2. As Frank Bidart reports Lowell did with *History*; Lowell, *Collected Poems*, p. 1074.

3. Christopher Ricks, *True Friendship* (New Haven: Yale University Press, 2010), p. 189.

4. A chance they were willing to take out of respect for Lowell, but also presumably because his books sold prolifically, and provided Lowell with a substantial income. Copies of his royalty statements from 1966 to 1970 can be found in Blair Clark's Robert Lowell Collection 1938–1983.

5. Erasmus to John Botzheim, 1523. *Opus Epistolarum Des. Erasmi Roterdami*, ed. P. S. Allen, vol. I, p. 27; quoted in Margaret Mann Phillips, *Erasmus on His Times: A Shortened Version of the Adages of Erasmus* (Cambridge: Cambridge University Press, 1967), p. xvii.

6. Lowell, "After Enjoying Six or Seven Essays on Me," p. 115; reprinted in Lowell, *Collected Poems*, p. 993.

7. Robert Lowell to Mrs. Robert Lowell [Elizabeth Hardwick], June 14, 1970, in *The Dolphin Letters*, p. 56.

8. Lowell, "A Note to the New Edition," *Notebook* (1970), p. 264.

This edition offers some hours of the pleasures of "living" different versions of the poems, not only the large changes Lowell made to the plot but delicate and distinct musical ones as well. Many of the poems wonder if his new life is an arrival or a departure, his doubts extending overtly outward in meaning, or inward in internal rhymes, as in the following lines from "Morning Blue" about facing the day:

> I am exposed, keeping[1] guessing if I can make
> the chill of the morning and put on my clothes.[2]

On the same manuscript page, he revised the rhyme:

> I am exposed, keep guessing if I can make
> the chill of the morning and its dressing.

Is the locution to "make | the chill of the morning" nautical—like making harbor, or making sail?[3] In the first version, the softening rhyme of "exposed" with "clothes" comes to a kind of arrival, at least in sound. The revised rhyme pairs "guessing" (by way of "morning") with "dressing," a feminine ending. Perhaps the change, both rhythmic and tonal, implies that covering himself for the day will not give him a morning's respite, nor put an end to his quandary.

In the final version, "make" is replaced with the perhaps more medicinal and bracing "take":

> I am exposed, keep guessing if I can take
> the chill of the morning and its dressing.[4]

It is in some of his smallest musical decisions that Lowell exposes and makes larger his meanings. "What is it that Eliot says, *Fare forward*? So we must."[5]

•

---

1. Thus, for "keep."
2. "Morning Blue" 3–4 [~~Marriage?~~ *Caroline* 4], "The Dolphin" manuscript.
3. Cf. "You are making Boston in the sulfury a.m." ("Old Snapshop from Venice 1952" 12 [*Hospital II* 3]).
4. "Morning Blue" 3–4 [*Caroline* 5].
5. Robert Lowell to Allen Tate, May 13, 1974, in *The Letters of Robert Lowell*, p. 629.

The publication of *The Dolphin* in 1973 was controversial. Many reviewers were uneasy with its claims of being "half fiction," and critiques, whether vehement or more equable, echoed the lines of argument made by those who had seen the prepublication version. "A lampooning!" Lowell wrote to Bishop. "\The/ distortion of the 'fictional' characters becomes a ~~kind~~ ~~of~~ slander on the people themselves [. . .] Your old letter of warning—I never solved the problem of the letters, and there and elsewhere of fact and fiction."[1] It is a coincidence of literary history that the reception of *The Dolphin* echoed arguments made against George Meredith's 1862 volume *Modern Love*, which was one of Lowell's models—a book of fifty adapted sonnets about the breakup of a marriage, in which "the actors are, it seems, the usual three: | Husband, and wife, and lover." *Modern Love* was excoriated in its time for being "graphic," a mere "common-place which is illustrated with a freedom that mistakes itself for courage, and is simply bad and prurient taste,"[2] for resembling "scattered leaves from the diary of a stranger" in an "obscure style"[3]—though also defended against "rash or partial attack," by a fellow poet, Swinburne.[4]

Alongside the controversy and gossip, *The Dolphin* had good reviews—one called it a "votive sculpture"[5]—and it won the 1974 Pulitzer Prize. Anthony Hecht, who served on the jury, praised it for having "a range of reference, dramatic leaps of movement and tone, an imaginative amplitude, that few could match. The poem on Freud, for example, and his family, is connected to Lowell and his own family in dense, complex and mortifying ways. The language is strong and plain, full of the resonance of heart-break; and alive with the capacity to reveal what the spirit has scarcely the courage to utter." William Alfred, another juror, confessed, "In all frankness, I was put off first reading the book by a certain callousness in the name of candor. I know the people involved. But

---

1. Robert Lowell to Elizabeth Bishop, July 12, 1973, in *The Dolphin Letters*, p. 360.

2. R. H. Hutton, "Mr. George Meredith's 'Modern Love,'" *The Spectator*, May 24, 1862, reprinted in George Meredith, *Modern Love and Poems of the English Roadside, with Poems and Ballads*, ed. Rebecca N. Mitchell and Criscillia Benford (New Haven: Yale University Press, 2012), pp. 182–83.

3. J. W. Marston, review in *Athenaeum*, May 31, 1862, reprinted in Mitchell and Benford, pp. 185–86.

4. Algernon C. Swinburne, letter to the editor, *The Spectator* (June 7, 1862), reprinted in Mitchell and Benford, p. 191.

5. Helen Vendler, "The Difficult Grandeur of Robert Lowell," *The Atlantic Monthly* (January 1975), reprinted in *Part of Nature, Part of Us: Modern American Poets* (Cambridge: Harvard University Press, 1980), p. 136.

on comparison with the other works nominated, I had no other choice but to cast my vote for it. It embodies an experience of our time, none the less tragic for being common; and it does so in a language worthy of the seriousness of that experience and supple enough to convey its desperately puzzling contradictions."[1]

A reader who pauses over this sequence of Lowell's poems to take in the arc of the whole book, or a set of lines, or an arresting image, or the "hundreds of aphorisms that stud and spice his poems,"[2] or the double meanings of his words ("common," "novel," and "plot"),[3] or the double meanings and several possible tones of his statements ("I have learned what I wanted"), will experience "the resonance of heart-break," the masterful capturing, in single gestures, of compounds and conjunctions of feeling and experience. Lowell wrote to Bishop in 1972, in the summer of further revising, and with his own poised rearrangement of Milton's words, "I'm trying to be simple sensuous and graceful."[4]

Saskia Hamilton

---

1. Ericka J. Fischer, *Chronicle of the Pulitzer Prizes for Poetry: Discussions, Decisions and Documents* (Berlin/Boston: Walter de Gruyter GmbH, 2010), pp. 320–21. Accessed July 3, 2018. ProQuest Ebook Central.

2. Michael Hofmann, "His Own Prophet," review of *Collected Poems* by Robert Lowell, edited by Frank Bidart and David Gewanter, *London Review of Books* 25, no. 17, September 11, 2003, p. 3.

3. See Steven Gould Axelrod, *Robert Lowell: Life and Art* (Princeton: Princeton University Press, 1978), p. 230.

4. Robert Lowell to Elizabeth Bishop, July 8, 1972, in *The Dolphin Letters*, p. 286.

# THE DOLPHIN

(1973)

*For Caroline*

# Fishnet

Any clear thing that blinds us with surprise,
your wandering silences and bright trouvailles,
dolphin let loose to catch the flashing fish. . . .
Poets die adolescents, their beat embalms them,
the archetypal voices sing offkey;
the old actor cannot read his friends,
and nevertheless he reads himself aloud,
genius hums the auditorium dead.
The line must terminate.
Yet my heart rises, I know I've gladdened a lifetime
knotting, undoing a fishnet of tarred rope;
the net will hang on the wall when the fish are eaten,
nailed like illegible bronze on the futureless future.

# Redcliffe Square

### 1. LIVING IN LONDON

I learn to live without ice and like the Queen;
we didn't like her buildings when they stood,
but soon Victoria's manly oak was quartered,
knickknacks dropped like spiders from the whatnot,
grandparents and their unmarried staffs decamped
for our own bobbed couples of the swimming twenties,
too giddy to destroy the homes they fled.
These houses, no two the same, tremble up six stories
to dissimilar Flemish pie-slice peaks,
shaped by constructor's pipes and scaffolding—
aboriginal like a jungle gym.
Last century's quantity brick has a sour redness
that time, I fear, does nothing to appease,
condemned by age, rebuilt by desolation.

### 2. WINDOW

Tops of the midnight trees move helter skelter
to ruin, if passion can hurt the classical
in the limited window of the easel painter—
love escapes our hands. We open the curtains:
a square of white-faced houses swerving, foaming,
the swagger of the world and chalk of London.
At each turn the houses wall the path of meeting,
and yet we meet, stand taking in the storm.
Even in provincial capitals,
storms will rarely enter a human house,
the crude and homeless wet is windowed out.
We stand and hear the pummelling unpurged,
almost uneducated by the world—
the tops of the moving trees move helter skelter.

### 3. AMERICA FROM OXFORD, MAY 1970

The cattle have stopped on Godstow Meadow,
the peacock wheels his tail to move the heat,
then pivots changing to a wicker chair,
tiara of thistle on his shitty bobtail.
The feathertouch of May in England, but the heat
is American summer. Two weeks use up two months;
at home the colleges are closed for summer,
the students march, Brassman lances Cambodia—
he has lost his pen, his sword folds in his hand like felt.
Is truth here with us, if I sleep well?—
*the ten or twelve years my coeval gives himself*
*for the new bubble of his divorce . . . ten or twelve years—*
this air so estranged and hot I might be home. . . .
We have climbed above the wind to breathe.


### 4. OXFORD

We frittered on the long meadow of the Thames,
our shoes laminated with yellow flower—
nothing but the soft of the marsh, the moan of cows,
the rooster-peacock. Before we had arrived,
rising stars illuminated Oxford—
the Aztecs knew these stars would fail to rise
if forbidden the putrifaction of our flesh,
the victims' viscera laid out like tiles
on fishponds changed to yellow flowers,
the goldfinchnest, the phosphorous of the ocean
blowing ambergris and ambergris,
dolphin kissing dolphin with a smirking smile,
not loving one object and thinking of another.
Our senses want to please us, if we please them.

## 5. THE SERPENT

In my dream, my belly was yellow, panels
of mellowing ivory, splendid and still young,
though slightly ragged from defending me.
My tan and green backscales were cool to touch.
For one who has always loved snakes, it is no loss
to change nature. My fall was elsewhere—
how often I made the woman bathe in her waters.
With daylight, I'd turn small, a small snake
on the river path, arrowing up the jags.
Like this, like this, as the great clock clangs round,
I see me—a green hunter who leaps from turn to turn,
a new brass bugle slung on his invisible baldric;
he is groping for trout in the private river,
wherever it opens, wherever it happens to open.


## 6. SYMPTOMS

A dog seems to lap water from the pipes,
a wheeze of dogsmell and dogcompanionship—
life-enhancing water brims my bath—
(the bag of waters or the lake of the grave. . . . ?)
from the palms of my feet to my wet neck—
I have no mother to lift me in her arms.
I feel my old infection, it comes once yearly:
lowered good humor, then an ominous
rise of irritable enthusiasm. . . .
Three dolphins bear our little toilet-stand,
the grin of the eyes rebukes the scowl of the lips,
they are crazy with the thirst. I soak,
examining and then examining
what I really have against myself.

## 7. DIAGNOSIS: TO CAROLINE IN SCOTLAND

The frowning morning glares by afternoon;
the gay world in purple and orange drag,
Child-Bible pictures, perishables:
oranges and red cabbage sold in carts.
The sun that lights their hearts lights mine?
I see it burn on my right hand, and see
my skin, when bent, is finely wrinkled batwing.
Since you went, our stainless steelware ages,
like the young doctor writing my prescription:
*The hospital.* My twentieth in twenty years. . . .
Seatrout run past you in the Hebrides—
the gay are psychic, centuries from now,
not a day older, they'll flutter garish colors,
salmontrout amok in Redcliffe Square.

# Hospital

## 1. SHOES

Too many go express to the house of rest,
buffooning, to-froing on the fringe of being,
one foot in life, and little right to that:
"I had to stop this business going on,
I couldn't attack my doctor anymore,
he lost his nerve for running out on life. . . ."
"Where I am not," we chime, "is where I am."
Dejection washes our pollution bare.
My shoes? Did they walk out on me last night,
and streak into the glitter of the blear?
I see two dirty white, punctured tennis-shoes,
empty and planted on the one-man path.
I have no doubt where they will go. They walk
the one life offered from the many chosen.


## 2. JUVENILIA

Person, place and thing, once violated,
join the rubbish that predated nature;
boys race the hooded highway lights untimed,
and tiptoe through the treasuries of smashed glass,
scavenging for a lifelike hand or head.
I hoped to find girls in the wide, white squares;
I had no names or numbers—I could not meet them,
the women had suffered a fate worse than death—
weird in London of the bullhorn God.
No rocket goes as far astray as man. . . .
I'm on bounds, I mark my proofs, a sheaf of tapeworms,
sleek, untearable, interminable
paper that slices my finger like a knife—
one time in fifty, God will make a date.

### 3. RIVAL

Is there an ur-dream better than words, an almost
work of art I commonplace in retelling
through the fearfullness of memory,
my perfunctory, all-service rhythms? . . .
For long, our taxi is changing into a van—
you-I . . . beefing we've not seen our driver.
He moves through the tan canvas-lapped bales of the van,
his step is careless, the bales begin to converge.
I am happy because I recognize
the man who assaulted you yesterday. . . .
Much later, the man's face, tan, a Chinese portrait,
floats symmetrical in a pool the same color.
It takes seconds to see the rival is dead,
the same water washes in and out of the mouth.


### 4. STAIRWELL

Climbing from chair to chair to chair to chair,
I dare not look the stairwell in the eye;
its underpinning soils like carbon paper,
each step up would stop an athlete's heart—
the stairwell is hollow, bored, unbearable,
the same six words repeating on a disk:
marching for peace with paranoia marching,
marching for peace with paranoia marching . . .
ever at my heels and stormily.
Darling, we have halved the ailing summer.
Did the beheaded wish himself in half?
He was so airily cool and free and high—
or did he wish the opposite like us,
when we stitched two summer months in one?

## 5. WALTER RALEIGH

Horseguard and Lifeguard, one loud red, one yellow,
colorful and wasteful and old hat. . . .
Americans can buy them on a postcard—
we do not see them with hallucinated eyes,
these horsemen, smartly antiqued and resurrected
from the blood of Crimea and Waterloo,
free to ramble London or trample France. . . .
Here sitting at your feet I feel no pressure
of analogies binding us to them.
Our omen is Raleigh kneeling for the axe—
he isn't going to die, it's not been painted.
Our Raleigh is a small boy in his velvet
and courting dress hearing an old buffer
lie about the toothless Spanish Main.


## 6. DOUBLE-VISION

I tie a second necktie over the first;
no one is always waiting at the door,
and fills the window . . . sometimes a Burmese cat,
or maybe my Daughter on the shell of my glasses.
I turn and see persons, my pajama top
loose-knotted on the long thin neck of a chair—
*make yourself at home.* The cat walks out—
or does it? The room has filled with double-shadows,
sedation doubles everything I see. . . .
You can't be here, and yet we try to talk;
somebody else is farcing in your face,
we haggle at cross-purposes an hour.
While we are talking, I am asking you,
"Where is Caroline?" And you *are* Caroline.

# Hospital II

## 1. VOICES

"What a record year, even for us—
last March, I knew you'd manage by yourself,
you were the true you; now finally
your clowning makes visitors want to call a taxi,
you tease the patients as if they were your friends,
your real friends who want to save your image
from this genteel, disgraceful hospital.
Your trousers are worn to a mirror. . . . That new creature,
when I hear her name, I have to laugh.
You left two houses and two thousand books,
a workbarn by the ocean, and two slaves
to kneel and wait upon you hand and foot—
tell us why in the name of Jesus." Why
am I clinging here so foolishly alone?


## 2. LETTER

"In London last month I encountered only
exhausted traffic and exhausting men—
the taxi driver might kill us, but at least he cared."
Cold summer London, your purer cold is Maine,
where each empty sweater and hollow bookcase hurts,
every pretext for their service gone.
We wanted to be buried together in Maine . . .
you didn't, "impractical, cold, out of touch."
The terrible postcards you bought and stamped for me
go off to Harriet, the Horseguards, the Lifeguards,
the Lord Mayor's Chariot, Queen Bess who could not bear—
true as anything else to fling a child. . . .
I shout into the air, my voice comes back—
nothing reaches your black silhouette.

### 3. OLD SNAPSHOT FROM VENICE 1952

From the salt age, yes from the salt age,
courtesans, Christians fill the churchyard close;
that silly swelled tree is a spook with a twig for a head.
Carpaccio's Venice is as wide as the world,
Jerome and his lion lope to work unfeared. . . .
In Torcello, the stone lion I snapped behind you,
*venti anni fa*, still keeps his poodled hair—
wherever I move this snapshot, you have moved—
it's twenty years. The courtesans and lions
swim in Carpaccio's brewing tealeaf color.
Was he the first in the trade of painting to tell tales? . . .
You are making Boston in the sulfury a.m.,
dropping Harriet at camp, Old Love,
Eternity, You . . . a future told by tealeaves.

# Caroline

## 1. FLASHBACK TO WASHINGTON SQUARE 1966

Two babies in your stroller, perhaps three,
all four of you in Bloomingdale polo coats;
they seemed to rush on one course, you another—
your brute joy in slanting them to the curb. . . .
We were Sunday people gone before we met.
We meet too many people, wives and husbands;
the family endures, the child is never weaned,
parents never err in guessing wrong. . . .
How mean the drink-money for the hour of joy,
its breathy charity and brag of body. . . .
I hesitate to argue for our love unloosed—
though we earn less credit than we burn,
joy in the moment crowns credulity,
dying to be what we are.

## 2. FRAGILITY

One foot in last year, one in last July,
the motionless month, the day that lasts a month.
We reach mid-journey, you lag by fifteen summers,
half a year more than Harriet's whole life.
The clock looks over my shoulder crazily.
This hospital is tinder . . . retards the sun,
melancholia sprinkles the blind root,
the cat nibbles little shoots foretelling rain,
sultry August is my wandering eye.
Hope grows less malign or thinks it might,
I wait for the hospital to catch on fire.
Keep me in your shadow . . . gold grizzling your undyed hair,
frail body of an athlete, her big hand—
your honor is humor and fragility.

### 3. JULY-AUGUST

In hospital I read the news to sleep:
the Fourth of July, Bastille Day, the 16th
your Birthday . . . my two-month bankholiday.
August is summer lost in England.
Green nettles prick the oversoil with acid,
eat up the vestiges of last summer's clearing. . . .
One simultaneous sickness was enough
for us. From Brighton to Folkestone, the heads lie prone,
the patients mend, the doctors die in peace,
plucking the transient artificial flower—
the father fails to mail a single lobster
or salty nude to prove his pilgrimage.
I have no one to stamp my letters . . . I love you,
a shattered lens to burn the clinging smoke.


### 4. MARRIAGE?

"I think of you every minute of the day,
I love you every minute of the day;
you gone is *hollow, bored, unbearable.*
I feel under some emotional anaesthetic,
unable to plan or think or write or feel;
*mais ca ira,* these things will go, I feel
in an odd way against appearances,
things will come out right with us, perhaps.
As you say, we got across the Godstow Marsh,
reached Cumberland and its hairbreadth Roman roads,
climbed Hadrian's Wall, and scared the stinking Pict.
Marriage? That's another story. We saw
the diamond glare of morning on the tar.
For a minute had the road as if we owned it."

## 5. MORNING BLUE

The bathwater honks in and in, ten minutes, twenty,
twists of fire and cooling jobless bubbles;
I am exposed, keep guessing if I can take
the chill of the morning and its dressing.
The bathroom is a daub of daylight,
the beefy, flustered pigeons swish their quills—
in time the pigeons will forget the window;
I cannot—I, in flight without a ledge.
Up the carpetted stairway, your shoes clack,
clack nearer, and absentmindedly withdraw,
life withdrawn like a bad lead in poker.
Life *is* withdrawn, but after all it will be. . . .
It's safer outside; in the open air,
the car flying forward to hit us, has room to swerve.

# Summer Between Terms

### 1.

The day's so calm and muggy I sweat tears,
the summer's cloudcap and the summer's heat. . . .
Surely good writers write all possible wrong—
are we so conscience-dark and cataract-blind,
we only blame in others what they blame in us?
(The sentence writes *we*, when charity wants *I*. . . .)
It takes such painful mellowing to use error. . . .
I have stood too long on a chair or ladder,
branch-lightning forking through my thought and veins—
I cannot hang my heavy picture straight.
I can't see myself . . . in the cattery,
the tomcats doze till the litters are eatable,
then find their kittens and chew off their breakable heads.
They told us by harshness to win the stars.

### 2.

Plains, trains, lorries simmer through the garden,
the reviewer sent by God to humble me
ransacking my bags of dust for silver spoons—
he and I go on typing to go on living.
There are ways to live on words in England—
reading for trainfare, my host ruined on wine,
my ear gone bad from clinging to the ropes.
I'd take a lower place, eat my toad hourly;
even big frauds wince at fraudulence,
and squirm from small incisions in the self—
they live on timetable with no time to tell.
I'm sorry, I run with the hares now, not the hounds.
I waste hours writing in and writing out a line,
as if listening to conscience were telling the truth.

# Fall Weekend at *Milgate*

1.

The day says nothing, and lacks for nothing . . . God;
but it's moonshine trying to gold-cap my life,
asking fees from the things I lived and loved,
pilgrim on this hard-edge Roman road.
Your portrait is fair-faced with your honesty,
the painter, your first husband, made girls stare.
Your wall mirror, a mat of plateglass sapphire,
mirror scrolls and claspleaves, shows this face,
huge eyes and dawn-gaze, rumination unruffled,
unlearning apparently, since 1952. . . .
I watch a feverish huddle of shivering cows;
you sit making a fishspine from a chestnut leaf.
We are at our crossroads, we are astigmatic
and stop uncomfortable, we are humanly low.

2.

The soaking leaves, green yellow, hold like rubber,
longer than our eyes glued to the window can take;
none tumble in the inundating air. . . .
A weak eye sees miracles of birth in fall,
I'm counterclockwise . . . did we fall
last April in London, late fifties in New York?
Autumn sops on our windshield with huge green leaves;
the seasons race engines in America
burying old lumber without truce—
leaf-blight and street dye and the discard girl . . .
the lover sops gin all day to solve his puzzle.
Nature, like philosophers, has one plot,
only good for repeating what it does well:
life emerges from wood and life from life.

3.

*Milgate* kept standing for four centuries,
good landlord alternating with derelict.
Most fell between. We're landlords for the weekend,
and watch October go balmy. Midday heat
draws poison from the Jacobean brick,
and invites the wilderness to our doorstep:
moles, nettles, last Sunday news, last summer's toys,
bread, cheeses, jars of honey, a felled elm
stacked like construction in the kitchen garden.
The warm day brings out wasps to share our luck,
suckers for sweets, pilots of evolution;
dozens drop in the beercans, clamber, buzz,
debating like us whether to stay and drown,
or, by losing legs and wings, take flight.

# Records

"... I was playing records on Sunday,
arranging all my records, and I came
on some of your voice, and started to suggest
that Harriet listen: then immediately
we both shook our heads. It was like hearing
the voice of the beloved who had died.
All this is a new feeling ... I got the letter
this morning, the letter you wrote me Saturday.
I thought my heart would break a thousand times,
but I would rather have read it a thousand times
than the detached unreal ones you wrote before—
you doomed to know what I have known with you,
lying with someone fighting unreality—
love vanquished by his mysterious carelessness."

# In Harriet's Yearbook

*You must be strong through solitude, said Fate,*
*for the present this thought alone must be your shelter—*
this in your yearbook by your photograph.
Your bearing is a woman's not full woman,
bent to a straw of grass just plucked and held
like an eyetest card—you mature in blacking out.
A girl can't go on laughing all the time.
The other campgirls sway to your brooding posture,
they too must scowl to see a blade of grass;
yet you are out of focus and blurred like me,
separation stoops and fogs the lens—
one more humiliation to blow away,
only husked out in monosyllable—
profundities too shallow to expose.

# Communication

"These communications across the sea,
but for once you were almost buoyant—
phone-conversations get so screwed . . . I wish
I had your lovely letter in my hand
delivered to me by the stately Alex
just the minute you hung up. I'm off
to Dalton to pick up Harriet's grades and record—
it is frightening to be a soul,
marked in the Book of Judgment once a month,
because you haven't lived much, and are alive.
Things go on, Pained Heart, another month is gone. . . .
She stayed up talking to us all last night,
giving three brainy women back their blast.
Age is nice . . . if that's your age . . . thirteen."

# Dream

For months the heat of love has kept me marching,
now I am healthy, and I cannot stand;
women see through me like a head of cheese.
Boys on a gold enamelled goiterband:
boys in ultra-violet tights and doublets,
from the costume shop of Botticelli,
albino Absaloms; they probe my thicket
with pikes and wingnets, and I try to breathe,
I try to keep up breathing when I hide.
This is not Florence, or German mercenaries;
this is England, main artery of fighting—mercy was murder
at Towton when King Edward's heralds counted
twenty thousand Lancastrian dead in the field,
doubling the number killed to make the count.

# Mermaid

1.

I have learned what I wanted from the mermaid
and her singeing conjunction of tail and grace.
Deficiency served her. What else could she do?
Failure keeps snapping up transcendence,
bubble and bullfrog boating on the surface,
belly lustily lagging three inches lowered—
the insatiable fiction of desire.
None swims with her and breathes the air.
A mermaid flattens soles and picks a trout,
knife and fork in chainsong at the spine,
weeps white rum undetectable from tears.
She kills more bottles than the ocean sinks,
and serves her winded lovers' bones in brine,
nibbled at recess in the marathon.


2.

Baudelaire feared women, and wrote, "Last night, I slept
with a hideous negress." Woe to Black Power,
woe to French women and the Academicians.
Why do I blush the moon with what I say?
Alice-in-Wonderland straight gold hair,
fair-featured, curve and bone from crown to socks,
bulge eyes bigger than your man's closed fist,
slick with humiliation when dismissed—
you are packaged to the grave with me,
where nothing's opened by the addressee . . .
almost a year and almost my third wife,
by accepting, by inviting, by surmounting,
rushing the music when the juice goes dead—
float like a butterfly and sting like a bee.

3.

Our meetings are no longer like a screening;
I see the nose on my face is just a nose,
your *bel occhi grandi* are just eyes
in the photo of you arranged as figurehead
or mermaid on the prow of a Roman dory,
bright as the morning star or a blond starlet.
Our twin black and tin Ronson butane lighters
knock on the sheet, are what they are,
too many, and burned too many cigarettes. . . .
Night darkens without your necessary call,
it's time to turn your pictures to the wall;
your moon-eyes water and your nervous throat
gruffs my directive, *"You must go now go."*
Contralto mermaid, and stone-deaf at will.


4.

I see you as a baby killer whale,
free to walk the seven seas for game,
warm-hearted with an undercoat of ice,
a nerve-wrung back . . . all muscle, youth, intention,
and skill expended on a lunge or puncture—
hoisted now from conquests and salt sea
to flipper-flapper in a public tank,
big deal for the Sunday ennui. . . . My blind love—
on the Via Veneto, a girl
counting windows in a glass café,
now frowning at her menu, now counting out
neanderthals flashed like shorebait on the walk. . . .
Your stamina as *inside-right* at school
spilled the topheavy boys, and keeps you pure.

5.

One wondered who would see and date you next,
and grapple for the danger of your hand.
Will money drown you? Poverty, though now
in fashion, debases women as much as wealth.
You use no scent, dab brow and lash with shoeblack,
willing to face the world without more face.
I've searched the rough black ocean for you,
and saw the turbulence drop dead for you,
always lovely, even for those who had you,
Rough Slitherer in your grotto of haphazard.
I lack manhood to finish the fishing trip.
Glad to escape beguilement and the storm,
I thank the ocean that hides the fearful mermaid—
like God, I almost doubt if you exist.

# The Mermaid Children

In my dream, we drove to Folkestone with the children,
miles of ashflakes safe for their small feet;
most coasts are sand, but this had larger prospects,
the sea drained by the out-tide to dust and dunes
blowing to Norway like brown paper bags.
Goodbye, my Ocean, you were never my white wine.
Only parents with children could go to the beach;
we had ours, and it was brutal lugging,
stopping, teasing them to walk for themselves.
When they rode our shoulders, we sank to our knees;
later we felt no weight and left no footprints. . . .
Where did we leave them behind us so small and black,
their transisters, mermaid fins and tails,
our distant children charcoaled on the sky?

# They

Why are women a fraction more than us?
Lie with a woman and wake with Liberation,
her bondage is our lash, her labor our dismissal.
Her witness bugles to my dubious shade:
*Woman victorious, animosity dead.*
(Will the worm turn and sting her victor heel?)
Stendhal knew women deserved an education:
"No civilization rests on its best men,
its highest level, the mothers of its children—"
no vacation from shepherding the lost children . . .
if a mother no longer cares for her children,
civilization sinks to its institutions,
says, "Your fucking little psychopaths,
I didn't ask for them, they came for me."

# The Friend

Your long arms antlered on the Goth-rude fireplace,
a frame ample and worthy of your wingspread . . .
whatever we say is for our hearts alone—
the first confidence of our two souls at school,
now seasoned with retrospective mercy.
Some meaning never has a use for words,
truth one couldn't tell oneself on the toilet,
self-knowledge swimming to the hook, then turning—
in Latin we learned no subject is an object.
*"You say you'll remarry, you can't take none or two. . . .*
All this makes me think of one thing, *you*,
at your age . . . think of it, it's the one big item
on your agenda—Do you really want
to live in the same room with anyone?"

# In the Mail

"Your student wrote me, if he took a plane
past Harvard, at any angle, at any height,
he'd see a person missing, *Mr. Robert Lowell.*
You insist on treating Harriet as if she
were thirty or a wrestler—she is only thirteen.
She is normal and good because she had normal and good
parents. She is threatened of necessity. . . .
I love you, Darling, there's a black black void,
as black as night without you. I long to see
your face and hear your voice, and take your hand—
I'm watching a scruffy, seal-colored woodchuck graze
on weeds, then lift his greedy snout and listen;
then back to speedy feeding. He weighs a ton,
and has your familiar human aspect munching."

# Doubt

## 1. DRAW

The cardtable is black, the cards are played face down,
black-backs on a black cloth; and soon by luck
I draw a card I wished to leave unchosen,
and discard the one card I had sworn to hold.
Dreams lose their color faster than cut flowers,
but I remember the number on my card,
a figure no philosopher takes to bed. . . .
Should revelation be sealed like private letters,
till all the beneficiaries are dead,
and our proper names become improper Lives?
Focus about me and a blur inside;
on walks, things nearest to me go slow motion,
obscene streetlife rushes on the wheelrim,
steel shavings from the vacillating will.


## 2. POINTING THE HORNS OF THE DILEMMA

From the dismay of my old world to the blank
new—water-torture of vacillation!
The true snakepit isn't monodrama Medea,
the gorgon arousing the serpents in her hair;
it's a room to walk with no one else, to walk,
take thought, unthink the thought and listen for nothing:
"She loves me too much to have my welfare at heart . . .
*they just aren't up to your coming home*
*three weeks, then leaving for a year. They just aren't.*
*They can't stand much more of anything,*
*they are so tired and hurt and worn. They go on,*
*knowing your real sickness is a fretful*
*deafness to little children . . . and suspect*
*it's impossible for anyone to help you."*

## 3. CRITIC

Is my doubt, last flicker of the fading thing,
an honorable subject for conversation?
*Do you know how you have changed from the true you?*
I would change my trueself if I could:
I am doubtful . . . uncertain my big steps.
I fear I leave many holes for a quick knife
to take the blown rose from its wooden thorns.
A critic should save her sharpest tongue for praise.
Only blood-donors retain the gift for words;
blood gives being to everything that lives,
even to exile where tried spirits sigh,
doing nothing the day because they think
imagination matures from doing nothing,
hoping for choice, the child of vacillation.

# Winter and London

## 1. CLOSED SKY

A hundred mornings greet the same closed sky,
one of nature's shows, one mantle wrapping
the dust of London with the dust of Europe—
in the interiors it is always night.
The clouds are welcome to us as insulation,
a silencer to the ultimate blue sky,
naked heaven's monologue with man.
In my country, the wettest Englishman
sparkles with approbation, magnifying
curious small things I could never see—
under closed sky, trifles are luminous,
gossip makes New York and London one,
one mouth . . . we use identical instruments
for putting up a house and pulling down.


## 2. AT *OFFADO'S*

The Latin Quarter abuts on Belgravia,
three floors low as one, blocks built of blocks,
insular eighteenth century laying down
the functional with a razor in its hand,
construction too practical for conservation.
An alien should count his change here, bring a friend.
Usually on weekend nights I eat alone;
you've taken the train for *Milgate* with the children.
At *Offado's*, the staff is half the guests,
the guitar and singers wait on table,
the artist sings things unconsolable:
"Girls of Majorca. Where is my Sombrero?
Leave me alone and let me talk and love me—
a cod in garlic, a carafe of cruel rosé."

## 3. FLOUNDER

In a day we pass from the northern lights
to doomsday dawns. Crowds crush to work at eight,
and walk with less cohesion than the mist;
the sky, without malice, is acid, Christmas lights
are needed to reveal the Thames. God sees—
wash me as white as the sole I ate last night,
acre of whiteness, back of Folkestone sand,
cooked and skinned and white—the heart appeased.
Soles live in depth, see not, spend not . . . eat;
their souls are camouflaged to die in dishes,
flat on their backs, the posture of forgiveness—
squinch-eyes, bubbles of bloodshot worldliness,
unable ever to turn the other cheek—
at sea, they bite like fleas whatever we toss.


## 4. MASTODON

They splashed red on the Jews about to be killed,
then ploughed them back and forth in captured tanks;
the wood was stacked, the chainsaw went on buzzing.
In the best of worlds, the jailors follow the jailed.
In some final bog, the mastodon,
curled tusks raised like trumpets to the sky,
sunk to their hips and armpits in red mud,
splashed red for irreversible liquidation—
the heavens were very short of hearing then.
The price of freedom is displacing facts:
gnashed tusk, bulk-bruised bulk and a red splash.
Good narrative is cutting down description;
nature sacrifices heightening
for the inevitable closing line.

## 5. FREUD

Is it honorable for a Jew to die as a Jew?
Even the German officials encouraged Freud
to go to Paris where at least he was known;
but what does it matter to have a following,
if no one, not even the concierge, says *good day*?
He took a house in London's amused humdrum
to prove that Moses must have been Egyptian—
"What is more monstrous than outliving your body?"
What do we care for the great man of culture—
Freud's relations were liquidated at Belsen,
Moses Cohn who had nothing to offer culture
was liquidated at Belsen. Must we die,
living in places we have learned to live in,
completing the only work we're trained to do?


## 6. HARRIET'S DONKEY

On this blank page no worse, not yet defiled
by my inspiration running black in type,
I see your sepia donkey laugh at me,
Harriet's doodle, me in effigy,
my passport photo to America
that enflames the soul and irritates the eye—
*M. de Maupassant va s'animaliser.*
Gloomier exiles brought their causes here,
and children crying up and down the stairs;
Freud found his statue, older Jewish prophets
bit in until their teeth had turned to chalk,
found names in London and their last persona,
a body cast up lifeless on this shore. . . .
Family, my family, why are we so far?

# During a Transatlantic Call

*We can't swing New York on Harry Truman incomes—*
the bright lights dragging like a ball and chain,
the Liberal ruined by the Liberal school.
*This was the price of your manic flight to London—*
the closed provincial metropolis, never
an asylum for the mercurial American mind. . . .
They say fear of death is a child's remembrance
of the first desertion. My daughter knows no love
that doesn't bind her with presents, letters, visits,
things outward and visible. . . . I've closed my mind
so long, I want to keep it closed, perhaps—
I have no faith in my right to will transcendence,
when a house goes, the species is extinct. . . .
They tell me to stop, they mustn't lose my money.

# Exorcism

**1.**

*What we love we are.* As November
hardens the morning hoarfrost, I grow small;
slowly the bridal fury shows white teeth,
parading in invisible link mail—
greenness slurs into sterility,
the landscape is New England textile gray.
You point your finger: *What you love you are.*
I know what it is for a woman to be left,
to wait in the ante-room of apprehension:
*Inasmuch as I am loved I am—*
a woman romanticizing her exorcist,
two souls in a cocoon of mystery.
*Your woman dances for you, child in arms,*
*she is dancing for you, Baby-Skull-Smile.*


**2.**

This morning, as if I were home in Boston, snow,
the pure witchery-bitchery of kindergarten winters;
my window whitens like a movie screen,
glaring, specked, excluding rival outlook—
I can throw what I want on this blank screen,
but only the show already chosen shows:
Melodrama with her stiletto heel
dancing bullet wounds in the parquet.
My words are English, but the plot is hexed:
one man, two women, the common novel plot.
what you love you are. . . .
*You can't carry your talent with you like a suitcase.*
*Don't you dare mail us the love your life denies;*
*do you really know what you have done?*

# Plotted

Planes arc like arrows through the highest sky,
ducks *V* the ducklings across a puckered pond;
Providence turns animals to things.
I roam from bookstore to bookstore browsing books,
I too maneuvered on a guiding string
as I execute my written plot.
I feel how Hamlet, stuck with the Revenge Play
his father wrote him, went scatological
under this clotted London sky.
Catlike on a paper parapet,
he declaimed the words his prompter fed him,
knowing convention called him forth to murder,
loss of free will and licence of the stage.
Death's not an event in life, it's not lived through.

# The Couple

"Twice in the past two weeks I think I met
Lizzie in the recurrent dream.
We were out walking. *What sort of street*, you ask,
*fair or London?* It was our own street.
*What did you hear and say?* We heard ourselves.
The sidewalk was two feet wide. We, arm in arm,
walked, squelching the five-point oakleaves under heel—
happily, they melted under heel.
Our manner had some intimacy in my dream.
*What were you doing on this honeymoon?*
Our conversation had a simple plot,
a story of a woman and a man
versifying her tragedy—
we were talking like sisters . . . you did not exist."

# Before Woman

## 1. BEFORE THE DAWN OF WOMAN

"Gazing close-up at your underjaw,
a blazon of barbaric decoration,
a sprinkle of black rubies, clots from shaving,
panting in measure to your wearied breath,
I see the world before the dawn of woman,
a jungle of long-horned males, their scab of rapine,
rhinoceros on Eden's rhinoceros rock. . . .
You hold me in the hollow of your hand—
a man is free to play or free to slack,
shifty past the reach of ridicule.
A woman loving is serious and disarmed,
she is less distracted than a pastured mare,
munching as if life depended on munching. . . .
Like the animals, I am humorless."

## 2. DAY

Even a green parrot can talk one book,
sing up his second-rate, most writers do;
Christians and women have thought all men are evil,
though nothing living wholly disappoints God.
Living with you is living a long book
*War and Peace*, from day to day to day,
unable to look off or answer my name.
My springless step still stalks for youngman's wildweed,
the goldfinch-nest defying euphemism,
the God-borne instant never letting up.
Where will you take me in the fizz of winter?
Darling, the cork, though fat and black, still pulls,
new wine floods our prehistoric veins—
the day breaks, impossible, in our bed.

# Artist's Model

1.

Hölderlin's thing with swan-scene and autumn
behind was something beautiful, wasn't it?
Manet's bottles mirrored behind his bar-girl
are brighter than the stuff she used to serve—
the canvas should support the artist's model.
Our children and theirs will have to pose for themselves;
we squeezed the juice, their job to eat the skin,
we put God on his knees, and now he's praying. . . .
When I sit in my bath, I wonder why
I haven't melted like a cube of sugar—
fiction should serve us with a slice of life;
but you and I actually lived what I have written,
the drunk-luck venture of our lives sufficed
to keep our profession solvent, was peanuts to live.

2.

"My cousin really learned to loathe babies,
she loved to lick the palate of her Peke,
as if her tongue were trying a liqueur—
what I say should go into your *Notebook*. . . .
I'd rather dose children on morphine than the churches.
When you are dying, and your faith is sick,
and you go on flapping in your sheets
like a cockroach fallen in a fishbowl;
you will look for the love you fumbled, and see
only religion caught naked in the searchlights—
Christians scream worse than atheists on the death-ward.
What is so infamous about it is
they shove your bed nearer the door to move the corpse;
you know damn well it isn't for fresh air."

3.

*"If it were done, twere well it were done quickly—*
to quote a bromide, your vacillation
is acne." And we totter off the strewn stage,
knowing tomorrow's migraine will remind us
how drink heightened the brutal flow of elocution. . . .
We follow our plot as timorously as actors,
unalterably divorced from choice by choice.
"If you woke and found an egg in your shoe,
would you feel you'd lost this argument?"
It's over, my clothes fly into your borrowed suitcase,
the good day is gone, the broken champagne glass
crashes in the ashcan . . . private whims, and illusions,
too messy for our character to survive.
I come on walking off-stage backwards.


4.

Our dream has been more than life is solid—
I touch your house, the price of the furniture,
the two round marble tables big as millwheels
in your parlor unvulgarized by clutter-comforts.
But I can say more than this about you,
equal your big eyes to a silver teaspoon,
hindsight cannot romance their anger away—
bite of dog or dolphin, laughing and meant.
In my dream of misinterpretation,
your midnight taxi meets the midnight train—
one person removed, the household falls askew
from the children's tea to toilet paper.
I read in the floorboards' unintelligible worm-script
the blanks for all our birthdays . . . yours by summer.

# Mermaid Emerging

The institutions of society
seldom look at a particular—
Degas's snubnosed dancer swings on high,
legging the toplights, never leaving stage,
enchanting lovers of art, discerning none.
Law fit for all fits no one like a glove. . . .
Mermaid, why are you another species?
"Because, you, I, everyone is unique."
Does anyone ever make you do anything?
"Do this, do that, do nothing; you're not chained.
I am a woman or I am a dolphin,
the only animal man really loves,
I spout the smarting waters of joy in your face—
rough weather fish, who cuts your nets and chains."

# Marriage

### 1. ANGLING

Withdrawn to a third your size, and frowning doubts,
you stare in silence through the afterdinner,
when wine takes our liberty and loosens tongues—
fair-face, ball-eyes, profile of a child,
except your eyelashes are always blacked,
each hair colored and quickened like tying a fly.
If a word amuses you, the room includes your voice,
you are audible; none can catch you out,
your flights are covered by a laughing croak—
a flowered dress lost in the flowered wall.
I am waiting like an angler with practice and courage;
the time to cast is now, and the mouth open,
the huge smile, head and shoulders of the dolphin—
I am swallowed up alive . . . I am.


### 2. TIRED IRON

Mulch of tired iron, bullet-stitch of straffing planes—
surely the great war of our youth was hollow;
still it had cleanness, now the smelly iron,
the war on reeds, the grand *noyades* of the rice-fields.
We promised to put back Liberty on her feet . . .
I can't go on with this, the measure is gone:
a waterfall, the water white on green,
like the white letters on my olive keyboard—
to stray with you and have you with me straying,
flesh of my body, saved by our severalness—
you will not marry, though disloyal to woman
in your airy seizures of submission,
preferring to have your body broken to being
unbreakable in this breaking life.

### 3. GRUFF

The sky should be clearing, but it cannot lighten,
the unstable muck flies through the garden trees,
there's morning in my heart but not in things.
We've almost made a marriage like our parents—
the poise of disaster! Our love means giving the wheel
a shake that scatters spurs of displaced bone
in the heel of the driver's hand; it means to turn
right angle on ourselves, on our external star.
We might have married as Christ says man must not
in heaven where marriage is not, and giving
in marriage has the curse of God and Blake.
I am in bondage here, and cannot fly;
when marriage is surmounted, what is left?
"Heaven, if such things are," you gruff into the phone.


### 4. LEAF-LACE DRESS

Leaf-lace, a simple intricate design—
if you were not inside it, nothing much,
bits of glinting silver on crinkled lace—
you fall perhaps metallic and as good.
Hard to work out the fact that makes you good,
whole spirit wrought from toys and nondescript,
though nothing less than the best woman in the world.
Cold the green shadows, iron the seldom sun,
harvest has worn her swelling shirt to dirt.
Agony says we cannot live in one house,
or under a common name. This was the sentence—
I have lost everything. I feel a strength,
I have walked five miles, and still desire to throw
my feet off, be asleep with you . . . asleep and young.

## 5. KNOWING

This night and the last, I cannot play or sleep,
thinking of Grandfather in his last poor days.
Caroline, he had such naked nights,
and brought his *tortures of the damned* to breakfast—
when his son died, he made his grandchildren plant trees;
his blood lives, not his name. . . . We have our child,
our bastard, easily fathered, hard to name . . .
illegibly bracketed with us. My hand
sleeps in the bosom of your sleeping hands,
firm in the power of your impartial heat.
I'm not mad and hold to you with reason,
you carry our burden to the narrow strait,
this sleepless night that will not move, yet moves
unless by sleeping we think back yesterday.


## 6. GOLD LULL

This isn't the final calm . . . as easily,
as naturally, the belly of the breeding
mother lifts to every breath in sleep—
*I feel tomorrow like I feel today*
in this gold lull of sleep . . . the muzzled lover
lies open, takes on the world for what it is,
a minute more than a minute . . . as many a writer
suffers illusions that his phrase might live:
*power makes nothing final, words are deeds.*
President Lincoln almost found this faith;
once a good ear perhaps could hear the heart
murmur in the square thick hide of Lenin
embalmed, wide-eyed in the lull that gives a mother
courage to be merciful to her child.

## 7. GREEN SORE

We wake too early, the sun's already up,
the too early chain-twitter of the swallows fatigues,
words of a moment's menace stay for life:
*not that I wish you entirely well, far from it.*
That was my green life, even heard through tears. . . .
We pack, leave *Milgate*, in a rush as usual
for the London train, leaving five lights burning—
to fool the burglar? Never the same five lights.
Sun never sets without our losing something,
keys, money—not everything. "Dear Caroline,
I have told Harriet that you are having a baby
by her father. She knows she will seldom see him;
the physical presence or absence is the thing."—
a letter left in a page of a book and lost.


## 8. LETTER

"I despair of letters. You say I wrote H. isn't
interested in the thing happening to you now.
So what? A fantastic untruth, misprint, something;
I meant the London scene's no big concern, just you. . . .
She's absolutely beautiful, gay, etc.
I've a horror of turmoiling her before she flies
to Mexico, alone, brave, half Spanish-speaking.
Children her age don't sit about talking *the thing*
about their parents. I do talk about you,
and I have never denied I miss you . . .
I guess we'll make Washington this weekend;
it's a demonstration, like all demonstrations,
repetitious, gratuitous, unfresh . . . just needed.
I hope nothing is mis-said in this letter."

## 9. HEAVY BREATHING

Your heavier breathing moves a lighter heart,
the sun glows on past midnight on the meadow,
willing, even in England, to stretch the day.
I stand on my head, the landscape keeps its place,
though heaven has changed. Conscience incurable
convinces me I am not writing my life;
life never assures which part of ourself is life.
Ours was never a book, though sparks of it
spotted the page with superficial burns:
the fiction I colored with first-hand evidence,
letters and talk I marketed as fiction—
but what is true or false tomorrow when surgeons
let out the pus, and crowd the circus to see us
disembowelled for our afterlife?


## 10. LATE SUMMER AT *MILGATE*

A sweetish smell of shavings, wax and oil
blows through the redone bedroom newly aged;
the sun in heaven enflames a sanded floor.
Age is our reconciliation with dullness,
my varnish complaining, *I will never die.*
I still remember more things than I forgo:
once it was the equivalent of everlasting
to stay loyal to my other person loved—
in the fallen apple lurked a breath of spirits,
the uninhabitable granite shone
in Maine, each rock our common gravestone. . . .
I sit with my staring wife, children . . . the dour Kent sky
a smudge of mushroom. In temperate years the grass
stays green through New Year—I, my wife, our children.

11. NINTH MONTH

For weeks, now months, the year in burden goes,
a happiness so slow burning, it is lasting;
our animated nettles are black slash
by August. Today I leaned through lunch on my elbows,
watching my nose bleed red lacquer on the grass;
I see, smell and taste blood in everything—
I almost imagine your experience mine.
This year by miracle, you've jumped from 38
to 40, joined your elders who can judge:
*woman has never forgiven man her blood.*
Sometimes the indictment dies in your forgetting.
You move on crutches into your ninth month,
you break things now almost globular—
love in your fullness of flesh and heart and humor.


12. QUESTION

I ask doggishly into your face—
dogs live on guesswork, heavens of submission,
but only the future answers all our lies—
has perfect vision. A generation back,
Harriet was this burdensome questionmark—
we had nowhere then to step back and judge the picture. . . .
I fish up my old words, *Dear* and *Dear Ones*;
the dealer repeats his waterfall of cards—
will the lucky number I threw down
come twice? Living is not a numbers game,
a poor game for a father when I am one. . . .
I eat, drink, sleep and put on clothes up here,
I'll get my books back when we've lived together—
in this room on which all other rocks bear down.

### 13. ROBERT SHERIDAN LOWELL

Your midnight ambulances, the first knife-saw
of the child, feet-first, a string of tobacco tied
to your throat that won't go down, your window heaped
with brown paper bags leaking peaches and avocados,
your meals tasting like Kleenex . . . too much blood is seeping . . .
after twelve hours of labor to come out right,
in less than thirty seconds swimming the blood-flood:
Little Gingersnap Man, homoform,
flat and sore and alcoholic red,
only like us in owning to middle-age.
"If you touch him, he'll burn your fingers."
"It's his health, not fever. Why are the other babies so pallid?
His navy-blue eyes tip with his head. . . . Darling,
we have escaped our death-struggle with our lives."


### 14. OVERHANGING CLOUD

This morning the overhanging clouds are piecrust,
milelong Luxor Temples based on rich runny ooze;
my old life settles down into the archives.
It's strange having a child today, though common,
adding our further complication to
intense fragility.
Clouds go from dull to dazzle all the morning;
we have not grown as our child did in the womb,
met Satan like Milton going blind in London;
it's enough to wake without old fears,
and watch the needle-fire of the first light
bombarding off your eyelids harmlessly.
By ten the bedroom is sultry. You have double-breathed;
we are many, our bed smells of hay.

## 15. CARELESS NIGHT

So country-alone, and O so very friendly,
our heaviness lifted from us by the night . . .
we dance out into its diamond suburbia,
and see the hill-crown's unrestricted lights—
all day these encroaching neighbors are out of sight.
Huge smudge sheep in burden becloud the grass,
they swell on moonlight and weigh two hundred pounds—
hulky as you in your white sheep-coat, as nervous to gallop. . . .
The Christ-Child's drifter shepherds have left this field,
gone the shepherd's breezy too predictable pipe.
Nothing's out of earshot in this daylong night;
nothing can be human without man.
What is worse than hearing the late-born child crying—
and each morning waking up glad we wake?


## 16. MORNING AWAY FROM YOU

This morning in oystery Colchester, a single
skeleton black rose sways on my flour-sack window—
Hokusai's hairfine assertion of dearth.
It wrings a cry of absence. . . . My host's new date,
apparently naked, carrying all her clothes
sways through the dawn in my bedroom to the shower.
Goodmorning. My nose runs, I feel for my blood,
happy you save mine and hand it on,
now death becomes an ingredient of my being—
my Mother and Father dying young and sixty
with the nervous systems of a child of six. . . .
I lie thinking myself to night internalized;
when I open the window, the black rose-leaves
return to inconstant greenness. A good morning, as often.

# Another Summer

A mongrel image for all summer, our scene at breakfast:
a bent iron fence of straggly wildrose glowing
below the sausage-rolls of new-mown hay—
Sheridan splashing in his blue balloon tire:
*whatever he touches he's told not to touch*
*and whatever he reaches tips over on him.*
Things have gone on and changed, the next oldest
daughter bleaching her hair three shades lighter with beer—
but if you're not a blonde, it doesn't work. . . .
Sleeping, the always finding you there with day,
the endless days revising our revisions—
everyone's wildrose? . . . And our golden summer
as much as such people can. When most happiest
how do I know I can keep any of us alive?


2. DOLPHINS
Those warmblooded watchers of children—*do not say*
*I have never known how to talk to dolphins,*
*when I try to they just swim away.*
We often share the new life, *the new life*—
I haven't stilled my New England shades by combing
the Chinese cowlicks from our twisted garden,
or sorted out the fluff in the boiler room,
or stumbled on the lost mouth of the cesspool.
Our time is shorter and brighter like the summer,
each day the chill thrill of the first day at school.
Coughs echo like swimmers shouting in a pool—
a mother, unlike most fathers, must be manly.
Will a second dachshund die of a misborn lung?
Will the burned child drop her second boiling kettle?

### 3. IVANA

Small-soul-pleasing, loved with condescension,
even through the cro-magnon tirades of six,
the last madness of child-gaiety
before the trouble of the world shall hit.
Being chased upstairs is still instant-heaven,
not yet tight-lipped weekends of voluntary scales,
accompanying on a recorder carols
rescored by the Sisters of the Sacred Heart in Kent.
Though burned, you are hopeful, experience cannot tell you
experience is what you do not want to experience.
Are teenagers the dominant of all ache?
Or flirting seniles, their conversation three noises,
their life-expectancy shorter than the martyrs?
How all ages hate another age,

and lifelong wonder what was the perfect age!


### 4. ALIMONY

   *(A Dream in the Future)*
3, 4, and then 5 children, fortunately
fortune's hostages and not all ours—
the sea comes in to us, we move it outward. . . .
I'm somewhere, nowhere; four Boston houses I grew from,
slash-brick expressionist New England fall;
I walk, run, gay with frost . . . with Harriet . . .
a barracuda settlement. (Santo Domingo,
quick divorces, solid alimony,
its dictator's marina unsafe because of sharks
checking in twice daily like grinning, fawning puppies
for our sewage, even for their own excrement. . . .)

"I am not sure I want to see her again."
Harriet laughing without malice . . . with delight:
"That's how mother talks about you."


5. THE NEW                    (CAROLINE)

The one moment that says, *I am, I am, I am.* . . .
My girlfriends tell me I must stay in New York,
one never has such new friends anywhere;
but they don't understand,
wherever he is is my friend.

# Leaving America for England

### 1. AMERICA

My lifelong taste for reworking the same water—
a day is day there, America all landscape,
ocean monolithic past weathering;
the lakes are oceans, nature tends to gulp. . . .
Change I earth or sky I am the same;
aging retreats to habit, puzzles repeated
and remembered, games repeated and remembered,
the runner trimming on his mud-smooth path,
the gamefish fattening in its narrow channel,
deaf to the lure of personality.
May the entertainment of uncertainty
help me from seeing through anyone I love. . . .
Overtrained for England, I find America . . .
under unmoved heaven changing sky.

### 2. LOST FISH

My heavy step is treacherous in the shallows—
once squinting in the sugared eelgrass for game,
I saw the glass torpedo of a big fish,
power strayed from unilluminating depth,
roaming through the shallows worn to bone.
I was seven, and fished without a hook.
Luckily, Mother was still omnipotent—
a battered sky, a more denuded lake,
my heavy rapier trolling rod bent *L*,
drowned stumps, muskrat huts, my record fish,
its endless waddling outpull like a turtle. . . .
The line snapped, or my knots pulled—I am free
to reach the end of the marriage on my knees.
The mud we stirred sinks in the lap of plenty.

### 3. TRUTH

Downstairs the two children's repeating piano duet,
*when truth says goodmorning, it means goodbye.*
The scouring voice of 1930 Oxford,
"Nothing pushing the personal should be published,
not even Proust's *Research* or Shakespeare's *Sonnets*,
a banquet of raw ingredients in bad taste. . . .
No Irishman can understate or drink. . . .
W. B. Yeats was not a gent,
he didn't tell the truth: *and for an hour,*
*I've walked and prayed*—who prays exactly an hour?
Yeats had bad eyes, saw nothing . . . not even peahens:
*What has a bard to do with the poultry yard?*
Dying, he dished his stilts, wrote one good poem,
small penance for all that grandeur of imperfection."


### 4. NO TELLING

*(For Caroline)*

How much less pretentiously, more maliciously
we talk of a close friend to other friends
than shine stars for his festschrift! Which is truer—
the uncomfortable full dress of words for print,
or wordless conscious not even no one ever sees?
The best things I can tell you face to face
coarsen my love of you in solitary.
See that long lonesome road? It must end
at the will and second of the end-all—
I am still a young man not done running around. . . .
The great circuit of the stars lies on jewellers' velvet;
be close enough to tell me when I will die—
what will love do not knowing it will die?
No telling, no telling . . . not even a last choice.

## 5. SICK

I wake now to find myself this long alone,
the sun struggling to renounce ascendency—
two elephants are hauling at my head.
It might have been redemptive not to have lived—
in sickness, mind and body might make a marriage
if by depression I might find perspective—
a patient almost earns the beautiful,
a castle, two cars, old polished heirloom servants,
Alka Seltzer on his breakfast tray—
the fish for the table bunching in the fishpond.
None of us can or wants to tell the truth,
pay fees for the over-limit we caught, while floating
the lonely river to senility
to the open ending. Sometimes in sickness,

we are weak enough to enter heaven.


## 6. FACING ONESELF

After a day indoors I sometimes see
my face in the shaving mirror looks as old,
frail and distinguished as my photographs—
as established. But it doesn't make one feel
the temptation to try to be a Christian.

# Foxfur

"I met Ivan in a marvelous foxfur coat,
his luxurious squalor, and wished you one . . . your grizzled
knob rising from the grizzled foxfur collar.
I long to laugh with you, gossip, catch up . . . or down;
and you will be pleased with Harriet,
in the last six months she's stopped being a child,
she says God is just another great man,
an ape with grizzled sideburns in a cage.
Will you go with us to *The Messiah*,
on December 17th, a Thursday,
and eat at the *Russian Tearoom* afterward?
You're not under inspection, just missed. . . .
I wait for your letters, tremble when I get none,
more when I do. Nothing new to say."

# On the End of the Phone

My sidestepping and obliquities, unable
to take the obvious truth on any subject—
why do I do what I do not want to say?
When nothing matters, I ask—I never know.
Your rapier voice—I have had so much—
hundred words a minute, piercing and thrilling . . .
the invincible lifedrive of everything alive,
ringing down silver dollars with each word. . . .
Love wasn't what went wrong, we kept our daughter;
what a good father is is no man's boast—
to be still friends when we're no longer children. . . .
Why am I talking from the top of my mouth?
I am talking to you transatlantic,
we're almost talking in one another's arms.

# Cars, Walking, etc., an Unmailed Letter

"In the last three days Sheridan learned to walk,
and left the quadruped behind—for some reason
small pets avoid him. . . ." Who shakes hands with a dead friend?
I see a huge, old rattling brown paper bag,
a picture, no fact; when I try to unwrap it,
it slips in my hands. It is our old car
resurrected from the must of negligence,
warning like Hector's Ghost from the underground—
the car graveyard . . . now no longer obsolete.
I do not drive in England, yet in my thought,
our past years, especially the summers, are places
I could drive back to if I drove a car,
our old Burgundy Ford station-wagon summer-car,
our fourth, and first not prone to accident.

# Flight to New York

### I. PLANE-TICKET

A virus and its hash of knobby aches—
more than ever flying seems too lofty,
the season unlucky for visiting New York,
for telephoning kisses transatlantic. . . .
The London damp comes in, its smell so fertile
trees grow in my room. I read Ford's *Saddest Story*,
his *triangle* I read as his student in Nashville.
Things that change us only change a fraction,
twenty-five years of marriage, a book of life—
a choice of endings? I have my round-trip ticket. . . .
After fifty so much joy has come,
I hardly want to hide my nakedness—
the shine and stiffness of a new suit, a feeling,
not wholly happy, of having been reborn.

### 2. WITH CAROLINE AT THE AIR-TERMINAL

"London Chinese gray or oyster gray,
every appalling shade of pitch-pitch gray—
no need to cook up far-fetched imagery
to establish a climate for my mood. . . .
If I have had hysterical drunken seizures,
it's from loving you too much. It makes me wild,
I fear. . . . We've made the dining-room his bedroom—
I feel unsafe, uncertain you'll get back.
I know I am happier with you than before.
Safer . . ." The go-sign blazes and my plane's
great white umbilical ingress bangs in place.
The flight is certain. . . . Surely it's a strange joy
blaming ourselves and willing what we will.
Everything is real until it's published.

### 3. PURGATORY

In his portrait, mostly known from frontispiece,
Dante's too identifiable—
behind him, more or less his height, though less,
a tower tapering to a fingerend,
a snakewalk of receding galleries:
Purgatory and a slice of Europe,
less like the fact, more like the builder's hope
It leans and begs the architect for support,
insurance never offered this side of heaven.
The last fifty years stand up like that;
people crowd the galleries to flee
the second death, they cry out manfully,
for many are women and children, but the maker
can't lift his painted hand to stop the crash.


### 4. FLIGHT

If I cannot love myself, can you?
I am better company depressed . . .
I bring myself here, almost my best friend,
a writer still free to work at home all week,
reading revisions to his gulping wife.
Born twenty years later, I might have been prepared
to alternate with cooking, and wash the baby—
I am a vacation-father . . . no plum—
flown in to New York. . . . I see the rising prospect,
the scaffold glitters, the concrete walls are white,
flying like Feininger's skyscraper yachts,
geometrical romance in the river mouth,
conical foolscap dancing in the sky . . .
the runway growing wintry and distinct.

## 5. NEW YORK AGAIN

After London, the wind, the eye, my thoughts
race through New York with gaping coarse-comb teeth,
the simple-minded streets are one-way straight,
no queues for buses and every angle right,
a cowering London with twenty times the soaring;
it is fish-shaped, it is modern, it is metal,
austerity assuaged with melodrama,
an irritable reaching after fact and reason,
a love of features fame puts up for sale—
love is all here, and the house desolate.
What shall I do with my stormy life blown towards evening?
No fervor helps without the favor of heaven,
no permissive law of nature picks up the bill—
survival is talking on the phone.


## 6. NO MESSIAH

Sometime I must try to write the truth,
but almost everything has fallen awry
lost in passage when we said goodbye in Rome.
Even the licence of my mind rebels,
and can find no lodging for my two lives.
Some things like death are meant to have no outcome.
I come like someone naked in my raincoat,
but only a girl is naked in a raincoat.
Planesick on New York food, I feel the old
Subway reverberate through our apartment floor,
I stop in our Christmas-papered bedroom, hearing
my *Nolo*, the non-Messianic man—
drop, drop in silence, then a louder drop
echoed elsewhere by a louder drop.

## 7. DEATH AND THE MAIDEN

Did the girl in *Death and the Maiden* fear marriage?
No end to the adolescence we attained
by overworking, then struggled to release—
my bleak habit of counting off minutes on my fingers,
like pages of an unrequested manuscript.
that brilliant onetime moment we alone shared,
the leftovers from God's picnic and old times.
Why do I weep for joy when others weep?
One morning we saw something, half weed, half wildflower,
rise from the only thruhole in the barn floor—
it had this chance in a hundred to survive.
We knew that it was someone in disguise,
a silly good person . . . thin, pealnosed, intruding,
the green girl who doesn't know how to leave a room.


## 8. NEW YORK

A sharper air and sharper architecture—
the old fashioned fishingtackle-box skyscrapers,
flesh of glass and ribs of tin . . . derisively
called *modern* in 1950, and now called modern.
As if one had tried to make polar bears
live in Africa—some actually survived,
curious, strong meat permutations of polar bear. . . .
It wasn't so once, O it wasn't so,
when I came here ten or twenty years ago. . . .
Now I look on it all with a yellow eye;
but the language of New Yorkers, unlike English,
doesn't make me fear I am going deaf. . . .
Last night at four or five, whenever I woke up,
I found myself crying—not too heavily.

### 9. SLEEPLESS

Home for the night on my ten years' workbed,
where I asked the facing brick for words, and woke
to my conscious smile of self-incrimination,
hearing then as now the distant, panting siren,
small as a harbor boat patrolling the Hudson,
persistent cry without diminishment
or crescendo through the sleepless hours.
I hear its bland monotony, the voice
that holds, and never shortcircuits the transcendence
I fiddled for imperiously and too long.
All my friends are writers. Do I deserve
to sleep, because I gave myself the breaks,
self-seeking with persistent tenderness
rivals seldom lavish on a brother?


### 10. NEW YORK

I can move around more . . . through the thirty years
to the New York of Jean Stafford, Pearl Harbor, the Church?
Most of my old friends are mostly dead,
entitled to grow infirm and lap the cream—
if time that hurt so much improved a little?
Our onslaught, not wholly Pyrrhic, to launch Harriet
on the heart-turning, now savage, megapolis. . . .
A friendly soft depression browns the air,
it's not my glasses needing a handkerchief . . .
it's as if I stood tiptoe on a chair
so that I couldn't help but touch the ceiling—
almost obscenely, complaisantly on the phone with
my three wives, as if three-dimensional space were my breath—
three writers, none New Yorkers, had their great years there.

## 11. CHRISTMAS

All too often now your voice is too bright;
I always hear you . . . commonsense, though verbal . . .
waking me to myself: truth, the truth, until
things are just as if they had never been.
*I can't tell the things we planned for you this Christmas.*
*I've written my family not to phone today,*
*we had to put away your photographs.*
*We had to.* We have no choice—we, I, they? . . .
Our Christmas tree seems fallen out with nature,
shedding to a naked cone of triggered wiring.
This worst time is not unhappy, green sap
still floods the arid rind, the thorny needles
catch the drafts, as if alive—I too,
because I waver, am counted with the living.


## 12. CHRISTMAS

The tedium and déjà-vu of home
make me love it; bluer days will come
and acclimatize the Christmas gifts:
redwood bear, lemon-egg shampoo, home-movie-
projector, a fat book, sunrise-red, inscribed
to me by Lizzie, "Why don't you lose yourself
and write a play about the fall of Japan?"
Slight spirits of birds, light burdens, no grave duty
to seem universally sociable
and polite. . . . We are at home and warm,
as if we had escaped the gaping jaws—
underneath us like a submarine,
nuclear and protective like a mother,
swims the true shark, the shadow of departure.

# Dolphin

My Dolphin, you only guide me by surprise,
forgetful as Racine, the man of craft,
drawn through his maze of iron composition
by the incomparable wandering voice of Phèdre.
When I was troubled in mind, you made for my body
caught in its hangman's-knot of sinking lines,
the glassy bowing and scraping of my will. . . .
I have sat and listened to too many
words of the collaborating muse,
and plotted perhaps too freely with my life,
not avoiding injury to others,
not avoiding injury to myself—
to ask compassion . . . this book, half fiction,
an eelnet made by man for the eel fighting—

my eyes have seen what my hand did.

# THE DOLPHIN
# MANUSCRIPT

(1972)

In this edition of *The Dolphin*, the 1972 and 1973 variants are presented from latest to earliest. This arrangement honors Lowell's decision to publish the book in and with its 1973 shape and plot.[1] In looking back over his art and the experiences from which it emerged, he revised away from the actual sequence of events toward the fictional.

Both versions frame and devise his experience. He asks compassion, classically, for "this book, half fiction," in his final poem, "Dolphin." Half fiction: the real and the fictional are pendant to each other. The characters bear the names of actual persons but the words they write or speak come through Lowell's hand or mouth. Their words are half Lowell's, inasmuch as he changed and transformed the sources he was working from, in document or memory. Of the poems featuring other voices, however much he sought to "blunt and angle" them in revision, this essential ventriloquy exists, in both the 1973 and the 1972 versions.

---

1. The 1973 first edition text of *The Dolphin* was superseded by the second printing and the 1974 paperback edition, and has long been unavailable. Lowell made more than a dozen changes to individual poems in the second printing. He made further changes to the paperback and for selections of his poems (in three editions, published in 1974, 1976, and 1977). His post-publication revisions are recorded in full in the editorially composite version of *The Dolphin* in the *Collected Poems*. In the 1973 first edition, there are on six occasions spellings or marks of punctuation that may well be typos, yet we cannot be certain. Lowell's subsequent changes to these may be his corrections or his revisions, so I thought it best to remain faithful throughout to the first edition without ruling on likelihoods.

As noted in this book's introduction, the major difference between the two states of the book is structural. The 1972 manuscript version closely follows the actual events as they unfolded in Lowell's life—the protagonist falls in love with Caroline, suffers a manic attack, recovers, vacillates, then, seven months later, flies to New York to end his marriage to Lizzie. The conception of Robert Sheridan,[1] his child with Caroline, comes in the dénouement. In the 1973 version, Lowell reorders the sequence of events and lengthens the stretch of time, making the protagonist's final decision to leave Lizzie for Caroline take place a year after the birth of the child, and marking a passage of time of more than two years. Lowell described his reasoning about the change in a letter:

> I had meant to end with the Flight to New York sequence, even after R. S.'s ~~birth~~ conception, but feared I would be lying. ~~Now~~ The "departure" is the real, though not chronological ending; it will of course seem to be *both* the real and chronological ending because I place it at the end—not from anything I say. Sophistry? No, not entirely. ~~It's~~ \This/ is the real truth of the story and is in a way happening again now. The letters are not really changed to improve—the most I can hope is to lose nothing . . . to both lose and gain.[2]

For Lowell, the "real truth of the story," retrospectively revealed, would admit these variations in plot, the gains and losses still in balance in the half fiction he was creating.

## A NOTE ON THE TEXT

Lowell completed a draft of *The Dolphin* in January 1972. As he worked toward the final version, he enlisted help from Caroline Blackwood and Frank Bidart. As Bidart recalls, they would review each page and Lowell, while "lying on his daybed, would dictate changes" for Blackwood or

---

1. The name given to the baby in *The Dolphin*, and also the true name of Robert Sheridan Lowell, Robert Lowell and Caroline Blackwood's son.

2. Robert Lowell to Frank Bidart, May 15, 1972, in *The Dolphin Letters*, p. 282.

Bidart to write on the page. The manuscript was finalized and copyedited by Bidart, who was preparing it for Lowell's friends to read, and possibly also "for a typist or printer."[1] If any change on a manuscript page was unclear, Bidart would rewrite it in the margins—but all changes are presumed to be Lowell's own.

This text, which Lowell never sanctioned for publication, is a facsimile of that early 1972 manuscript, intended to be experienced as Lowell's friends did when it was circulated to them. Its typescript is clear and legible, while the writings in the margins offer a visual impression of Lowell's work on the page. Lowell's rewordings are transcribed for clarity and given inside the whole line, to allow readers to hear the line's full rhythm and pattern of sounds. Handwritten changes and corrections are inserted in the place indicated in the line. Those in Lowell's hand are transcribed in roman type; those he dictated to Frank Bidart, Caroline Blackwood, and in one instance perhaps an unknown other, are transcribed in *italic* type, with the initials of the scribe given in italicized brackets (*[FB]* for Frank Bidart, *[CB]* for Caroline Blackwood). Any hand-corrected typographical errors, as well as changes to punctuation, are recorded. Changes of mind (erased pencilings, revisions reconsidered) are given twice, in ~~canceled~~ and uncanceled versions. The typist's overstrikes are transcribed only if they seem to indicate a suggestive revision or change of mind. In two instances, marginal changes (made in the last seven pages of the manuscript, from Frank Bidart's photocopy; see below) are illegible.

The manuscript is assembled from two sources. Lowell's original typescript with marginal changes is at the Harry Ransom Center at the University of Texas at Austin, and consists of pages 1 to 50, except for a missing title page and page 25. The title page, page 25, and the final pages, numbered 51 to 58, come from Frank Bidart's photocopy. We can be confident that the manuscript reproduced in this edition is the version given to Lowell's friends in early 1972, with no evidence that Lowell introduced any new changes to the recto[2] pages of his copy after Bidart photocopied it.

Print standardizes handwritten changes in ways that can make the lexical field busy—it is no substitute for the typescript itself, which reveals

---

1. Interview with editor, January 29, 2017.
2. The versos of six manuscript pages contain writing—in one instance, notes toward a poem not part of *The Dolphin*; in four others, mistyped titles. They are not reproduced in this edition. Bidart's corrections to section 2 of *Artist's Model*, on page 38, run to the verso, and are here included.

most clearly Lowell's processes of composition and revision, and which an attentive, interested reader can experience readily with transcriptions as an aid to understanding.

My gratitude to Catherine Barnett, Jonathan Galassi, Paul Keegan, Emily Kramer, Christopher Ricks, and Fiona Wilson for their generosity of attention and, always, their essential discernment.

<sup>THE</sup> DOLPHIN

by

Robert Lowell

THE DOLPHIN

by

Robert Lowell

# CONTENTS

WINTER AND LONDON:                                    [2]
   1. CLOSED SKY
   2. AT <u>OFFADO'S</u>
   *3. FLOUNDER*                                    *[FB]*

   ~~3.~~<sup>4.</sup> MASTODON     4
   ~~4.~~<sup>5.</sup> FREUD
   ~~5.~~<sup>6</sup> HARRIET'S DONKEY
TRANSATLANTIC CALL
EXORCISM I--~~3~~ <sup>2</sup>   ~~3?~~
PLOTTED
THE COUPLE
THE ARTIST'S MODEL I--3
MERMAID EMERGING
MARRIAGE ?:
   1. ANGLING
   2. TIRED IRON
   3. LEAF-LACE
   4. GRUFF
   5. MARRIAGE?
BEFORE WOMAN:~~?:~~                                   *[FB]*
   1. BEFORE THE DAWN OF WOMAN
   2. DAWN
~~SICKDAY:~~ *LEAVING AMERICA FOR ENGLAND*            *[FB]*
   1. LEAVING AMERICA FOR ENGLAND?
   2. LOST FISH
   3. SICKDAY
FLIGHT TO NEW YORK:
   1. FOX-FUR
   2. <u>THE MESSIAH</u>
   3. PLANE TICKET
   4. *Departure* AT THE AIR TERMINAL                *[FB]*
   5. FLIGHT
   6. NEW YORK AGAIN
   7. NO MESSIAH
   8. SLEEPLESS
   9. CRISTMAS 1970
   10. CHRISTMAS 1970

WINTER AND LONDON:
    I. CLOSED SKY
    2. AT OFFADO'S     ← 4.   3. FLOUNDER
    4. 3. MASTODON
    3. 4. FREUD
    6 5. HARRIET'S DONKEY
TRANSATLANTIC CALL
EXORCISM I--3 2
PLOTTED
THE COUPLE
THE ARTIST'S MODEL I--3
MERMAID EMERGING
MARRIAGE ?:
    I. ANGLING
    2. TIRED IRON
    3. LEAF-LACE
    4. GRUFF
    5. MARRIAGE?
BEFORE WOMAN;?:
    I. BEFORE THE DAWN OF WOMAN
    2. DAWN
SICKDAY: LEAVING AMERICA FOR ENGLAND
    I. LEAVING AMERICA FOR ENGLAND?
    2. LOST FISH
    3. SICKDAY
FLIGHT TO NEW YORK:
    I. FOX-FUR
    2. THE MESSIAH
    3. PLANE TICKET
    4. AT THE AIR TERMINAL   Departure
    5. FLIGHT
    6. NEW YORK AGAIN
    7. NO MESSIAH
    8. SLEEPLESS
    9. CRISTMAS I970
    I0. CHRISTMAS I970

~~THE~~ BURDEN:

1. KNOWING
2. QUESTION
3. OVERHANGING CLOUD
4. GOLD LULL
5. GREEN SORE
6. "Indespair of letters..."

6.[7.] LATER WEEK AT <u>MILGATE</u>
7.[8] NINE MONTHS
8.[9] MORNING AWAY FROM YOU
9.[10] ROBERT SHERIDAN

DOLPHIN

~~THE~~ BURDEN:
1. KNOWING
2. QUESTION
3. OVERHANGING CLOUD
4. GOLD LULL
5. GREEN SORE      6. "I despair of letters..."
7. ~~6~~. LATER WEEK AT <u>MILGATE</u>
8. ~~7~~. NINE MONTHS
9. ~~8~~. MORNING AWAY FROM YOU
10. ~~9~~. ROBERT SHERIDAN

DOLPHIN

FIRST FISHNET

1   Any clear thing that holds up the reader,‾

4   The heights are hollow; robers <sup>robbers</sup> pry the gold          [FB]

6–8   his archi<sup>e</sup>typal girth. Summer, summer,          [FB]
      poets die adole<sup>s</sup>cents, their beat embalms them,          [FB]
      the survivor stops read<sup>ing</sup> French, his friends, the news,

## ~~FIRST~~ FISHNET

Any clear thing that holds up the reader,—
the line must terminate, the bright trouvaille,
the glitter of the viking in the icecap.
The heights are hollow; robers pry the gold    *robbers*
from the fine print and volume of the colossus,
his archetypal girth. Summer, summer,
poets die adolecents, their beat embalms them,
the survivor stops read/French, his friends, the news, *in*
and nevertheless can read himself aloud;
genius hums the auditorium dead...
My heart rises, I know I've gladdened a lifetime
knotting a fishnet of tarred rope,
the net will hang on the wall when the fish are eaten,
nailed like illegible bronze to the futureless future.

## [REDCLIFFE SQUARE]

I. ~~The~~ Window

10    a storm$^{s}$ will rarely enter a human house,

[2. America from Oxford, Spring 1970]

2    the peacoock wheels his tail to move the heat,

8    the students march, the Brass lances Cambodia, ⁻

10    Is truth here not there, if we ~~still~~ <sup>can</sup> sleep,

12    hasn't ~~yet~~ <sup>evolved</sup> to us . . . this heat that moves

REDCLIFFE SQUARE

I. ~~The~~ Window

Tops of moving trees move helter skelter
to ruin, if news can hurt the classical
innthe limited window of the easel painter----
love escapes our hands. We pull the curtains:
a crescent of white-faced houses swerving, foaming,
the swagger of the world and chalk of London.
At each turn the houses wall the path of meeting,
and yet we meet, stand taking in the storm.
Even in less civilized centers,
a storm will rarely enter a human house,
the crude and homeless wet is windowed out.
We stand and hear the pummelling unpurged,
almost uneducated by the world----
the tops of the moving trees move helter skelter.


2. America from Oxford, Spring I970

The cattle have stopped on the Godstow Meadow,
the peacock wheels his tail to move the heat,
then pivots changing to a wicker chair,
tiara of thistle on his shitty bobtail.
The feather-touch of May in England, but the heat
is American summer. Two weeks use up two months;
at home the colleges are closed for summer,
the students march, the Brass lances Cambodia,
he has lost his pen, his sword folds in his hand like felt.
Is truth here not there, if we still sleep, *can*
Bystander? The peacock spins, the Revolution
hasn't evolved to us...this heat that moves
air so estranged and hot we might be home...
We have walked above the wind to breathe.

[(Redcliffe Square)]

[3. Oxford]

1    We frittered $^{on}$ the long meadow till ~~are~~ $^{our}$ shoes

6    the Aztecs knew the star$^s$ would fail to rise

14    Our sen$^s$es want to please us, if we please them.


[4. The Serpent]

4    ~~though~~ mellowing too near $^{the}$ life-end like myself.

6    to change nature, My fall was elsewhere—

11    I see me⁄ ... ~~T~~$^t$he $^{I\,see\,me\,...\,the}$ green hunter leaps from turn to turn, $^{[FB]}$

14    wherever it opens, wher$^n$ever it happens to open.

(Redcliffe Square)

3. Oxford

We frittered ~~the~~ the long meadow till ~~are~~ shoes *[ON]* *[OUR]*
were laminated with its yellow flower.
Nothing but dung of the marsh, the moan of cows,
the machismo of the peacock. Before we arrived,
rising stars illuminated Oxford---
the Aztecs knew the star would fail to rise
without putrifaction of our flesh,
the victims' viscera inlaid on the fishpond,
and changed to yellow flowers, to meadows, stars,
the goldfinchnest, the phosphorous of the ocean
blowing ambergris and ambergris,
dolphin kissing dolphin with smirking smile,
not loving one object and thinking of another.
Our senes want to please us, if we please them. *[S]*

4. The Serpent

In my dream, my belly was yellow, panels
of mellowing ivory, splendid and still young;
my tan and green backscales were cool to touch,
~~though~~ mellowing too near life-end like myself. *[THE]*
For one who has always loved snakes, it is no loss
to change nature. My fall was elsewhere---
how often I made the woman bathe in her waters.
With daylight, I turn small, a small snake
on the river path, darting up the jags.
Like this, as often as the great clock clangs round,
I see me...the green hunter leaps from turn to turn, *[I see me ... the]*
a new brass bugle slung on his invisible baldric;
he is groping for trout in the private river,
wherever it opens, wherever it happens to open. *[N]*

[(Redcliffe Square)]

[6. Diagnosis: a Letter to Caroline in Scotland]

5    The sun that lights their ha$^e$arts lights mine?

7    the skin, when bent, is finely wrinkled ~~wrinkled~~ batwing.

(Redcliffe Square)

5. Symptoms

A dog seems to lap water from the pipes,
glowing with dogsmell and companionship,
and life-enhancing water brims the tub
from the palms of my feet to my wet neck,
from the bag of waters to the lake of the grave.
I have no mother to take me in her arms.
I feel my old infection, it comes yearly:
lowered good humor, then an ominous
rise of irritable enthusiasm...
Three dolphins bear our little toilet-stand,
the grin of the eyes denies the scowl of the lips,
they are crazy with the thirst. I soak,
examining and then examining
what I really have against myself.


6. Diagnosis: a Letter to Caroline in Scotland

The frowning morning is glare-afternoon;
the gay world in purple and orange drag
are like a children's Bible, perishables:
oranges and red cabbage sold in carts.
The sun that lights their hearts lights mine?
I see the sun on my right hand, and see
the skin, when bent, is finely wrinkledbw~~wrinkled~~ batwing.
Since you went, the stainless steel has aged
and the young doctor writing my prescription:
The hospital. My twenty in twenty years...
Seatrout run past you in the Hebrides---
the gay are psychic, centuries from now,
not a day older, they'll flash their garish colors,
salmontrout amok in Redcliffe Square.

*between 7 and 8*

HOSPITAL

1. Shoes

Too many go express to the house of rest,
sighing, to-froing on the fringe of being,
one foot in life, and little right to that:
"I had to stop this business going on,
I couldn't attack my doctor anymore,
he had no thought of the voyage back to life..."
"Where I am not," they chime, "is where I am."
Dejection washes our pollution bare.
My shoes? Did they walk out on me last night,
streak into the glitter of the blear?
I see two dirt-white, riddled tennis-shoes,
empty and planted in my oneway road.
There is no doubt where they will go.  They walk
the one life offered from the many chosen.

⟨HOSPITAL⟩

1². The Stairwell

1    Climbing from chair to chair to ᶜhair to chair,

4    each step up the stairwell athletes's heart—

11–14  ~~Do~~ <sup>Did</sup> the beheaded wish ~~to break in two?~~ himself in half?
~~They are~~ <sup>He was</sup> so air͒ly *airily* cool and free and high‿’
~~Or do they ask for unity like us,~~
A foot pointed downward, the other nowhere..‥—

before we stitched tʷo summer months in one?

(HOSPITAL)

### 2. The Stairwell

Climbing from chair to chair to chair to chair,
I dare not look the stairwell in the eye;
the underpinning is carbon paper and corks,
each step up the stairwell athletess heart---
the stairwell, hollow, bore, unbearable,
the same six words repeated on a disk:
marching for peace with paranoia marching,
marching for peace with paranoia marching...
ever at my heels and stormily.
Darling, we have halved the ailing summer.
Do the beheaded wish to break in two?
They are so airly cool and free and high,
Or do they ask for unity like us,
before we stitched to summer months in one?

*Did*

*Himself in back.*

*airily*

*h*

*He was*

*a foot pointed downward, the other nowhere*

[(Hospital)]

3. ²·³ Juvenilia        [FB]

4–5   and tiptoe through the ^its treasures of smashed glass,
      spooky guaze-heads, ^and skeletons of form.

7–11  I hope^d to find girls in the wide, white night;
      ~~I have^d no names or numbers—the town~~ ^London ~~; is~~ ^was is was ~~weird;~~
      ~~No rocket went~~ ^goes ~~astray as far~~ ^astray ~~as man;~~
      ~~I am not in danger, if I dope~~ ^feed stay indoors; ~~and rest,~~ ^here;
      ~~sorting out my~~ ^my my ~~galleys, a gaggle of tapeworms;~~        [FB]

          *I had no name or numbers—London is weird,*        [FB]

          *a gray wolf howling to his bullhorn god.*        [FB]

          *No rocket goes as far astray as man,....*        [FB]

          *I have stayed home sorting my galleys, a gaggle of tapeworms,*        [FB]

13    paper that slices my fingers like a knife—

4. ³·⁴ Double-Vision        [FB]

4–7   or maybe ^my Mother on the shell of my glasses.
      When I turn I w^see my pajama top
      loose-knotted on the long thing neck of a chair—
      make yourself at home. The cats walks out—

9–12  ~~librium~~ ^sedation doubling^es everything I see ...
      You can't be here, ‾and yet we try to talk;
      ~~an earlier love~~ ^somebody else is farcing ~~with~~ ^in your face,
      we ~~gabble~~ ^haggle at cross-purpose^s ~~half~~ an hour.

96

3, 3. Juvenilia

Person, place and thing, once violated,
fall back on the rubbish that predated nature;
boys race untimed along the hooded highway,
and tiptoe through the treasures of smashed glass, *ITS*
spooky guaze-heads, ˄skeletons of form.  *AND*
Meeting danger is like meeting a person unknown.
I hope˄to find girls in the wide, white night;
~~I had no names or numbers——the town is weird,~~ *LONDON IS* 
~~No rocket went astray as far as man;~~ *GOES*
~~I am not in danger, if I dope and rest,~~ *FEED  STAY INDOORS*
~~sorting out my~~ galleys, a gaggle of tapeworms, *MY*
sleek, untearable, interminable,
paper that slices my fingers like a knife———
one time in fifty, God will make a date.


4, 4.Double-Vision

I knot a second necktie over the first;
no one is always waiting at the door,
or in a window...sometimes a Manx cat,
or maybe˄Mother on the shell of my glasses. *MY*
When I turn I see my pajama top            *SEE*
loose-knotted on the long thin neck of a chair———
**make yourself at home.** The cat walks out———
or does it? The room is filled with double-shadows,
~~librium~~ doubling everything I see...  *SEDATION*
You can't be here; and yet we try to talk... *IN*
~~an earlier level~~ is farcing with your face,
we gabble at cross-purposes ~~half~~ an hour. *SOMEBODY ELSE*
While we are talking, I am asking you,       *HAGGLE*
"Where is Caroline?" And you __are__ Caroline.


I had no name or numbers — London is weird,
a gray wolf howling to his bullhorn god.
No rocket goes as far astray as man....
I have stayed home sorting my galleys, a gaggle of
                                              tapeworms,

## [THE FARTHER SHORE]

### [I. From my Wife]

5–8   bore, bore the friends who ~~want to keep~~ <sup>wished to save</sup> your image
      from ~~your~~ <sup>this</sup> genteel, disgraceful hospital.
      You tease the sick as if their<sup>y</sup> were your friends;
      your suit <sup>is</sup> lazies<sup>d</sup> to grease. And that new woman—

11–12   a workbarn by the ocean, and a ~~woman~~ <sup>slave</sup>
      ~~who~~ <sup>to</sup> kneels and waits ~~on~~ <sup>upon</sup> (stet) on you hand and foot—

14   are you clinging <sup>t</sup>here <sup>*there*</sup> so foolishly from us?"     *[FB]*

### 2. Old ~~Family~~ Snapshot and Carpaccio

4–5   Carpaccio's Venice ~~is was~~ <sup>was</sup> as wide as the world,
      Jerome and his lion ~~scoot~~ <sup>loped</sup> to work unfeared . . .

7–9   <u>venti anni fa</u>, still ~~poodles his~~ <sup>*keeps his poodled*</sup> hair—   *[CB]*
      wherever ~~you~~ <sup>I</sup> moved your snapshot, he has moved <sup>on,</sup>
      <sup>for</sup> twenty years. The saint and animal

11   the first in the trade of painting to tell tales~~? . . .~~ <sup>? . . . *[3 dots after question*</sup>
                                           *mark]* *[FB]*

14   eternity, ~~us, you,~~ <sup>~~you and us,~~ you and us,</sup> mothbitten time.

THE FARTHER SHORE

I. From my Wife

"What a record year, even for us---
last March, we hoped you'd manage by yourself,
you were the true you; now finally
your clowning makes us want to vomit---you bore,
bore, bore the friends who want to keep your image  *WISHED TO SAVE*
from your genteel, disgraceful hospital.  *THIS*
You tease the sick as if they were your friends;
your suit, lazied to grease. And that new woman---  *is*
when I hear her name, I have to laugh.
You have left two houses, two thousand books,
a workbarn by the ocean, and a woman  *SLAVE*
*TO* who kneels and waits on you hand and foot---  *upon (s 767)*
tell us why in the name of Jesus. Why
are you clinging here so foolishly from us?"  *there*

2. Old Family Snapshot and Carpaccio

From the salt age, yes from the salt age,
courtesans, Christians fill the barnyard close;
that silly swelled tree is a spook with a skull for a cap.
Carpaccio's Venice was wide as the world,  *was*
Jerome and his lion scout to work unfeared...  *LOPED*
In Torcello, the lion snapped behind you,  *Keeps his poodled*
venti anni fa, still poodles his hair---
wherever you moved your snapshot, he has moved on,  *I*
*A* twenty years. The saint and animal  *FOR*
swim Carpaccio's tealeaf color. Was he
the first in the trade of painting to tell tales?/..  *[3 dots after question mark]*
You are making Boston in the early A.M.,
dropping Harriet at camp, old love,
eternity, us, mothbitten time.
        *YOU AND US,*
        *YOU AND US,*

[(The Farther Shore)]

[3. Notes for an unwritten Letter]

1–3    Ice ~~of first autumn~~ <sup>in the air</sup>, enough to make me hold
my ~~feet~~ <sup>socks</sup> for warmth. A purer cold in Maine—
all things are truer there, truth~~'s~~ <sup>is a</sup> foreign language.

5    ~~are mailed~~ <sup>have gone</sup> to Harriet: the horseguards, the lifeguards,

8–10    In Maine, my country ~~as I loved to boast,~~ <sup>where I</sup> ~~hoped~~ <sup>wished</sup> to die,
each empty sweater and ~~vacant~~ <sup>idle</sup> bookshelf hurts,
~~the~~ <sup>all the</sup> pretexes for their service gone.

14    Is a sound sleeper one ~~you~~ <sup>who</sup> will not wake?

3. Notes for an unwritten Letter

Ice ~~of first autumn~~, enough to make me hold
[IN THE AIR]
[Socks] my ~~feet~~ for warmth. A purer cold in Maine--- [IS A]
all things are truer there, truth's/foreign langauge.
The terrible postcards you bought and stamped for me
~~are mailed,~~ to Harriet: the horseguards, the lifeguards,
the golden Lord Mayor's chariot, Queen Bess--- [HAVE GONE]
true as anything else to fling a child...
[WISHED]
In Maine, my country ~~as I loved to boast,~~ WHERE I ~~HOPED~~ TO DIE,
each empty sweater and ~~vacant~~ bookshelf hurts, [IDLE]
~~the~~ pretexes for their service gone.   [ALL THE]
I shout into the air, my voice comes back,
it doesn't carry to the farther shore,
rashly removed, still ringing in my ears.
Is a sound sleeper one ~~you~~ will not wake?
                    WHO

~~MARRIAGE?~~ Caroline

[I. Flashback to Washington Square 1966]

7    the ~~drain keeps on~~ *loss* endures, the child is never weaned,    *[CB]*


2. ~~Frailty~~ Fragility

2    the motionless months, the day *that* lasts a month.

4    about as long as I ~~have~~ held *on* ~~my~~ *to* marriage.

7    it*s* cat nibbles little shoots foretelling rain,

10–13    The hospital is tinder, and very nervous.

Hope grows less malign or thinks it might—
~~only this one person, never the other.~~
You lend me your shadow. Gold grizzles your undyed hair,

~~The air is tinder. Gold grizzles your undyed hair,~~
frail ~~boy~~ *body* of an athlete, her big hand,

~~MARRIAGE?~~ *CAROLINE*

I. Flashback to Washington Square 1966

Two babies in your stroller, perhaps three,
all four of you in matching polo coats;
they seemed to rush on one course, you another---
your brute joy in slanting them to the curb...
We were Sunday people gone before we met.
We meet too many people, wife and husband,
*loss* the ~~drain keeps on~~, the child is never weaned, *ENDURES*
parents never err in guessing wrong...
How mean the drink-money for the hour of joy,
its breathy charity and brag of body...
I hesitate to argue for love unloosed,
but surely it cuts the toll more than men count---
joy in the moment crowns credulity,
dying is becoming what we are.


2. ~~Frailty~~ *FRAGILITY*

One foot in August, one in last July,
the motionless months, the day lasts a month. *THAT*
We reach mid-journey, you lag by fifteen summers,
about as long as I ~~have~~ held ~~my~~ marriage. *ON TO*
The clock looks over my shoulder crazily.
The hospital retards the sun, and burns,
it's cat nibbles little shoots foretelling rain,
melancholia sprinkles the blind root,
sultry August is a wandering eye.
Hope grows less malign or thinks it might---
~~only this one person, never the other.~~
The ~~air is tinder.~~ Gold ~~grizzles your undyed hair,~~
frail boy of an athlete, her big hand,
honor in your humor and fragility.

*BODY*

*THE HOSPITAL IS TINDER, AND VERY NERVOUS.*
*YOU LEND ME YOUR SHADOW. GOLD GRIZZLES YOUR*
*UNDYED HAIR,*

[(Marriage?)]

[3. July-August]

1     In hospital I<sub>∧</sub>read the news <sup>to</sup> ~~a~~sleep:

6–9    eat up the vestiges of ~~love's old path~~— <sup>last year's faith,</sup>
one simul<sup>t</sup>aneous sickness is enough.
From Brighten to St. Tropez, the heads lie prone,
the patients mends' the doctors die in peace,

11–12  ~~voyagers who fail to save a single~~ <sup>tourist who failed</sup>
<sub>tourists who failed to save a single saline</sub>

~~saline~~ nude or <sup>sunset</sup> lobster to prove their travels.

[4. Morning Blue]

4     the chill of the morning<sub>∧</sub>and ~~put on my clothes~~. <sup>and its dressing.</sup>

7–8    The pigeons will in time forget the window;<sup>s;</sup>
I cannot—man ~~is~~ in flight without a ledge.

10    thump nearer, ~~and neglectively retreat,~~ <sup>then and absent-mindedly withdraw,</sup>

(Marriage?)

3. July-August

In hospital I read the news, asleep: *TO*
the Fourth of July, Bastile Day, your Birthday;
the Revolution's on bank holiday.
August is summer lost in England.
Green nettles prick the oversoil with acid,
eat up the vestiges of ~~leaves old path~~ — *LAST YEAR'S FAITH,*
one simultaneous sickness is enough.
From Brighten to St. Tropez, the heads lie prone,
the patients mend, the doctors die in peace,
plucking the transient artificial flower---
~~voyagers who fail to save a single~~ *TOURIST WHO FAILED*
~~saline~~ nude or lobster to prove their travels. *SUNSET*
I have no friend to write to...I love you,
a shattered lens to burn the clinging smoke.
*TOURISTS WHO FAILED TO SAVE A SINGLE SALINE*

4. Morning Blue

The bathwater honks in, ten minutes, twenty,
twists of ice and burning jobless bubbles;
I am exposed, keep guessing if I can make
the chill of the morning and ~~put on my clothes.~~ *AND ITS DRESSING.*
Beafy, flustered pigeons sound their quills
in the shadeless windows, daubs of daylight.
The pigeons will in time forget the window *; ;*
I cannot---man is in flight without a ledge. *WITHDRAW,*
Up the carpeted stairway, your shoes thump, *AND ABSENT-MINDEDLY*
thump nearer, ~~and neglectively retreat,~~ *THEN*
life withdrawn like a bad lead in poker.
Life _is_ withdrawn, but after all it will be...
It's safer outside; in the open air,
the car flying forward to hit us, glides behind.

## [SUMMER BETWEEN TERMS]

out   [CB]

2–4 the reviewer sent by God to humble me,
ransacking my bags of dust for his silver spoon'
*to keep on typing just to go on living.* [FB]


7–9 ~~my ears flattened by clinging to the ropes,~~
a vibrance in the sinew and fat of my legs.
I'd take a lower ~~road,~~ place *place* eat my toad hourly; [FB]


13 ~~I s<sup>p</sup>end~~ I've spent a a morning writing back ten words,

## SUMMER BETWEEN TERMS

Plains, trains, traffic simmer through the garden,
the reviewer sent by God to humble me.
ransacking my bags of dust for his silver spoon,
There must be ways of making a living in England---
reading for trainfare, my host ruined on wine,
~~my ears flattened by clinging to the ropes,~~
~~a~~ vibrance in the sinew and fat of my legs.
I'd take a lower road, eat my toad hourly;    *a sure place*
even big frauds wince at fraudulence,
and squirm from small incisions in the self---
they live on timetable with no time to tell.    *I've spent*
~~I s~~end a morning writing back ten words,
as if listening to conscience were telling the truth.
I'm sorry, I run with the hares now, not the hounds.

*to keep on typing just to go on living.*

[FALL WEEKEND AT <u>MILGATE</u>]

[I.]

5–6    Your portrait glowers with sincer*e*ᶦty,                    [*FB*]
       the painter, your husband, always made ~~you~~ ᵍⁱʳˡˢ stare.

9–12   your rose-glaze will not ruffle, ~~a portrait~~ ⁻⁻⁻ ᵗʰᵉ ᵖⁱᶜᵗᵘʳᵉ unchanged,
       unlearning appara*e*ntly, since 1950. ··                    [*FB*]
       ~~Fall already looks further along than it is,~~
       *Here* a huddle of shivering cows and feverish leaves‿      [*FB*]
       *burying old lumber without truce.*                         [*FB*]


[2.]

4–10   warm with rainbow and false fires of spring,· *[period]*    [*FB*]
       ~~burning old lumber without truce.~~
       *Weak eyes see miracles of birth in fall,*                  [*FB*]

       I ' am counterclockwise; we first met
       last April in London, ᵒʳ late fifties in New York?
       ~~A~~ ᵞᵒᵘʳ ʸᵒᵘʳ face ten years unchanged in my ~~weak eyes.~~ ᵈᵃʳᵏ ˢⁱᵍʰᵗ.
       The seasons r~~a~~ace engines in America;                   [*FB*]
       ~~a~~ ᵗʰᵉ ᵗʰᵉ lover sops gin all day to solve h*is* puzzle;  [*FB*]

FALL WEEKEND AT <u>MILGATE</u>

I.

The day sees nothing, misses nothing...God.
It's moonshine hoping to regild our lives,
asking grace of things we lived and loved,
pilgrims on this hard-edge Roman road.
Your portrait glowers with sincerity,          *GIRLS*
the painter, your husband, always made you stare.
Your wall mirror in a mat of plateglass sapphire
shows the same face, the huge eyes and dawn-stare;
your rose-glaze will not ruffle, a ~~portrait~~ unchanged, *IN THE PICTURE*
unlearning apparently, since 1950. ~~. . .~~
~~Fall already looks further along than it is,~~
*Here* a huddle of shivering cows and feverish leaves
We are at the astigmatic crossroads,
and stop uncomfortable, we are humanly low.

2.                    *burying old lumber without truce.*

The soaking leaves, green yellow, hold like rubber,
longer than our eyes glued to the window can take;
none tumble in the inundating air,
warm with rainbow and false fires of spring~~,~~. *[period]*
~~burning old lumber without truce.~~
I ~~am~~ counterclockwise; we first met       *OR*
last April in London, ~~l~~late fifties in New York?
*Your* ~~A~~ face ten years unchanged in my ~~weak eyes~~. *YOUR DARK SIGHT.*
The seasons r~~a~~ace engines in America;
*THE* ~~a~~ lover sops gin all day to solve his puzzle;  *THE*
summer sops on our windshield with huge green leaves...
Nature, like philosophers, has one plot,
only good for repeating what it does well:
life emerges from wood and life from life.

*Weak eyes see miracles of birth in fall,*

[Fall Weekend at Milgate]

[3.]

3      Most fell between. We're landlords of <sup>for</sup> the weekend,

(Fall Weekend at Milgate)

3.

<u>Milgate</u> kept standing for four centuries,
good landlord alternating with derelict.    *FOR*
Most fell between. We're landlords ~~at~~ the weekend,
and watch October go balmy. Midday heat
draws poison from the Jacobean brick,
and invites the wilderness to our doorstep:
moles, nettles, last Sunday news, last summer's toys,
bread, cheeses, jars of honey, a felled elm
stacked like construction in the kitchen garden.
The warm day brings out wasps to share our luck,
suckers for sweets, pilots of evolution;
dozens drop in the beercans, clamber, buzz,
debating like us whether to stay and drown,
or, by losing legs and wings, take flight.

["I was playing records"]


11    than all the detached unreal one$^s$ you wrote before—

"I was playing records"


"Dearest, I was playing records on Sunday,
arranging all my records, and I came
on some of your voice, and started to sugest
that Harriet listen: then immediately
we both shook our heads. It was like hearing
the voice of the beloved who had died.
All this was a new feeling...I got the letter
this morning, the letter you wrote me Saturday.
I thought my heart would break a thousand times,
but I would rather have read it a thousand times
than all the detached unreal ones you wrote before---
you doomed to know what I have known with you,
lying with someone fighting unreality---
love vanquished by his mysterious carelessness."

## [HARRIET'S YEARBOOK]

1–3   <u>"You must be strong through solitude," said Fate,</u>    *[FB]*

      <u>"For the present this though~~t~~ alone must be your shelter.</u>"="":

      is ~~is put~~ *thus* in your yearbook by your photograph.    *[CB]*

14    profundties too shallow to expose,    *[FB]*

HARRIET'S YEARBOOK

"You must be strong through solitude," said Fate,
"For the present this though alone must be your shelter—"
is in your yearbook by your photograph.
Your bearing is a woman's not full woman,
bent to a straw of grass just plucked and held
like an eyetest---mature in blacking out.
A girl can't go on laughing all the time.
The other campgirls sway to your brooding posture,
they too must scowl to see a blade of grass;
yet you are out of focus and blurred like me,
separation stoops and fogs the lens---
one more humiliation to blow away,
only husked out in monosyllable---
profundties too shallow to expose,

## [COMMUNICATION]

6    just the minute you hung up. I'm off ~~to~~

8    it ~~'s~~ <sup>is</sup> frightening ~~for a child~~ to be a soul,

10–11  because you ~~are alive and~~ haven't lived ~~. . .~~, and are alive.
    Things go on, Pained Heart, ~~October's~~ a month is gone . . .

COMMUNICATION

"Your communications across the sea,
Dear, for once you were almost bouyant---
phone-conversations get so screwed...I wish
I had your lovely letter in my hand
delivered to me by the stately Alex
just the minute you hung up. I'm off to
to Dalton to pick up Harriet's grades and record---
*15* it's frightening ~~for a child~~ to be a soul,
marked in the Book of Judgment once a month, *AND ARE ALIVE*
because you ~~are alive and~~ haven't lived. *A MONTH IS*
Things go on, Pained Heart, ~~October's~~ gone...
She stayed up talking to us all last night,
giving three brainy women back their blast.
Age is nice...if that's your age...thirteen."

# [PURGATORY]

~~out~~      [CB]

10    The last ~~sixty~~ <sup>fifty</sup> years stand up like that;

~~19. The Hunt~~[1] <sup>My Goiter</sup>

*separate poem*      [FB]

2–3    now I am <sup>so</sup> healthy, ~~and~~ <sup>and</sup>I can~~not~~ <sup>not</sup> stand;
        ~~But~~ wo~~man~~ sees through me like a head of cheese—

4    see enamelled on ~~the~~ <sup>my</sup> gold goiter band

9    I try to keep up breathing ~~while~~ <sup>when</sup> I hide.

---

1. From the sequence *May* in *Notebook* (1970).

PURGATORY

In his portrait, mostly known from frontispiece,
Dante's too identifiable---
behind him, more or less his height, though less,
a tower tapering to a palmsbreadth point,
a snakewalk of receding galleries:
Purgatory and a slice of Europe,
less like the fact, more like a builder's model.
It leans and begs the builder for support,
insurance never offered this side of heaven.
The last sixty years stand up like that;  *FIFTY*
people crowd the galleries to flee
the second death, they cry out manfully,
for many are women and children, but the maker
can't lift his painted hand to stop the crash.

## The Hunt  *Garisa*

For months the poison of love has kept me marching,
now I am healthy, and I cannot stand;
women see through me like a head of cheese—
see enamelled on the gold goiter band  *my*
men from the costume shop of Botticelli,
men in ultra-violet tights and doublets,
coiffures of Absolom; they probe my thicket
with pikes and swingnets, and I try to breathe,
I try to keep up breathing while I hide.  *WHEN*
These are not Tuscan or Roman mercenaries;
this is England, main artery of fighting—mercy was murder,
at Towton when King Edward's heralds counted
twenty thousand Lancastrian dead in the field,
doubling the number as they made the count.

*separate poem*

## [MERMAID]

### [1.]

5     bubble and bullfrog boating on the se$^u$rface,         *[FB]*

10–12 ~~and leaves a cone of skin and mist behind.~~
     *weeps white rum undetectable from tears.*      *[FB]*

    A mermaid pastures on the dews of $^h$eaven;     *[FB]*
    she has killed more bottles than the c$^o$cean,     *[FB]*

### [2.]

6     fair-featured, curve and bone' from crown to socks,     *[FB]*

13–14  rushing the music when the juice goes dead. ⁻     *[FB]*
    I̶ feel$^{ing}$ tomorrow like I feel today.

MERMAID

I.

I have learned what I wanted from the mermaid
and her singeing conjunction of tail and grace.
Deficiency served her. What else could she do?
Failure keeps snapping up transcendence,
bubble and bullfrog boating on the surface,
belly lustily lagging three inches lowered.
None swims with her and breathes the air.
A mermaid flattens soles and picks a trout,
knife and fork in chainsong at the spine,
and leaves a cone of skin and mist behind.
A mermaid pastures on the dews of heaven;
she has killed more bottles than the ocean,
and serves her winded lovers' bones in brine,
nibbled at recess in the marathon.


2.

Baudelaire feared women, and wrote, "Last night, I slept
with a hideous negress."  Woe to Black Power,
woe to the French Academy and scribe.
Why do we blush the moon with what we say?
Alice-in-Wonderland straight gold hair,
fair-featured, curve and bone, from crown to socks,
bulge eyes bigger than your man's closed fist,
slick with humiliation when dismissed---
you are packaged to the grave with me,
where nothing's opened by the addressee...
almost a year and almost my third wife,
by accepting, by inviting, by surmounting,
rushing the music when the juice goes dead,
I feel tomorrow like I feel today.
                ing

weeps white rum undetectable from tears.

[(Mermaid)]

[3.]

13    Your stamina as <u>inside-right</u>_at school

[4.]

1     Our meeting^s are no longer like a screening;

8     knock on the sheet, are what the^y are,                    *[CB]*

11    it's time to take your picture from the ~~shelf~~ *wall*;    *[CB]*

13–14  gruffs my directive, "~~You must go now go~~ <u>You must go now go.</u> "
       ^My Contralto mermaid' ~~and~~ *and* stone-deaf at will.      *[CB]*

3.

I see you as a baby killer whale,
free to walk the seven seas for game,
warm-hearted with an outercoat of ice,,
a nerve-wrung back, all muscle, youth, intention,
and skill expended on a lunge or puncture---
hoisted now from conquests and salt sea
to flipper-flapper in a public tank,
big deal for weekend children and blind love...
On the Via Veneto, a girl
sat counting windows in a glass cafe,
now frowning at her menu, now counting out
neanderthals flashed like shorebait on the walk...
Your stamina as _inside-right_ at school
spilled the topheavy boys, and keeps you pure.


4.

Our meeting are no longer like a screening;
I see the nose on my face is just a nose,
your _belli occhi grandi_ are just eyes
in the photo of you arranged as figurehead
or mermaid on the prow of a Roman dory,
bright as the morning star or a blond starlet.
Our twin black and tin Ronson butane lighters
knock on the sheet, are what they are,
too many, and burned too many cigarettes...
Night darkens without your necessary call,
it's time to take your picture from the ~~shelf~~ wall;
your moon-eyes water and your nervous throat
gruffs my directive, "_You_ must _go_ now _go_."
Contralto mermaid, ~~and~~ and stone-deaf at will.

[(Mermaid)]

[5.]

3    Will money drown you? ~~Yet~~ <sup>P</sup>poverty debases

6    will<sup>ing willing</sup> to face the world without a face.

10    Rough Slitherer in ~~the~~ <sup>your</sup> grotto of haphazard.

(Mermaid)

5.

I've wondered who would see and date you next,
and grapple in the aspic of your flesh.
Will money drown you? ~~But~~ /poverty debases
women as much as wealth, though not for vogue.
You use no scent, and dab your eyes with shoeblack,
will to face the world without a face.    *WILLING*
I've searched the rough black ocean for you,
and saw the turbulence drop dead for you,
always lovely, even for those who had you,
Rough Slitherer in t~~he~~ grotto of haphazard.  *YOUR*
I lack manhood to finish the fishing trip.
Glad to escape beguilement and the  storm,
I thank the ocean that hides the fearful mermaid---
like God, I almost doubt if you exist.

# [THE MERMAID CHILDREN]

1    In ^my dream, I drove to Folkestone for our children,

4    the out-tide ~~had~~ drained the sea to dust and dune

10–12  They rode our shoulders, we sank ~~in~~ ^down to our knees;
later we felt no burden, ~~had~~ ^left no footprints . . .
Where ~~are~~ ^were they left behind, so small and black,

THE MERMAID CHILDREN

In /dream, I drove to Folkestone for our children,
miles of ashland safe for their small feet;
most coasts are sand, but this had drier prospect,
the out-tide had drained the sea to dust and dune
blowing to Norway like brown paper bags.
Goodbye, my Ocean, you were never my white wine.
Only parents with children were let in;
we had ours, and it was brutal lugging,
stopping, begging them to walk for themselves.
They rode our shoulders, we sank in to our knees;
later we felt no burden, had no footprints...
Where are they left behind, so small and black,
their transister, mermaid fins and tails,
our distant children charcoaled on the sky?

*(handwritten annotations: "My" above "dream"; "Down" right of "themselves."; "LEFT" right of "footprints..."; "were" right of "black,")*

[WOMEN]

1. [FB]

1    Why are ~~they~~ *you they you* a fraction more than us? [FB]

4    Their witness ~~bulges~~ *bugles* to my dubious shade: [FB]

6–7    w<sup>*W*</sup>hat worm ~~wild~~ turns on the victor and stings her heel?
                                  *This line inserted before "Stendahl" line –* [FB]

Steandhal knew women deserved an education:

                                   OUT    [FB]

                                             [FB]

2.

1–14  ~~Father directed choir. When it paused on Sundays,~~
      ~~he liked to loiter the morning with the girls;~~
      ~~then back to cottage, dinner cold on the table.~~
      ~~Mother locked in bed and eating tabloid.~~
      ~~You should see him, white fringe about his ears,~~
      ~~bald skull, less bias than a billiard ball =~~
      ~~he never left a party. Once when Mother left first,~~
      ~~I threw myself from the car and broke my leg . . .~~
      ~~I missed him, I missed Mother's cold silence more =~~
      ~~years later, he said, "How jolly of you to jump."~~
      ~~When I am unhappy, I try to stretch the hour~~
      ~~and hour or half-hour sooner than it is;~~
      ~~orphaned, I wake at four and pray for night =~~
      ~~lovely ladies have helped me through the day.~~

WOMEN

Why are they, a fraction more than us?
Lie with a woman and wake with Liberation,
lash of bondage and the pangs of labor.
Their witness bulges to my dubious shade;    bulges
Woman victorious, animosity dead.
Steandhal knew women deserved an education:
"No civilization rests on its best men,
its highest level, the mothers of its children."
A vacation from shepherding the lost children——
what worm will turns on the victor and sting her heel?
If a mother no longer cares for her children,
civilization sinks to its institutions,
it says, "Your fucking little psychopaths,
I didn't come for them, they came for me."

OUT

Father directed choir. When it paused on Sundays,
he liked to loiter the morning with the girls;
then back to cottage, dinner cold on the table,
Mother locked in bed and eating tabloid.
You should see him, white fringe about his ears,
bald skull, less bone than a billiard ball——
he never left a party. Once when Mother left first,
I threw myself from the car and broke my leg...
I minded him, I missed Mother's cold silence more——
years later, he said, "How jolly of you to jump."
When I am unhappy, I try to stretch the hour
and hour or half-hour sooner than it is;
orphaned, I wake at four and pray for night——
lovely ladies have helped me through the day.

*you*

*this line inserted before "Steandhl" line —*

# [THE FRIEND]

2    a frame ample and worthy of your wingsp$^r$ead . . .     *[FB]*

5–7   seasoned with the mercy of retro$^s$pect.     *[CB]*
      Some ~~calls never have a~~ <sup>meaning never finds its</sup> way with words,
      truths one ~~could~~ <sup>couldn't</sup> tell one's-self on the toilet,

10–11  "I have to may$^r$ry, I'm not up to two."
      "All this makes me think of one thing' ~~you~~<sup>you</sup>,

14    to live in the same room ~~as~~ <sup>with</sup> anyone?"

THE FRIEND

Your long arms antlered on the Goth-rude fireplace,
a frame ample and worthy of your wingspead...
whatever we say is for our hearts alone---
first confidence of our two souls at school,
seasoned with the mercy of retropect.
Some ~~calls never have a~~ way with words, *MEANING NEVER FINDS ITS*
truth~~s~~ one ~~could~~ tell one's-self on the toilet, *COULCON'T*
self-knowledge swimming to the hook, and turning---
in Latin we learned no subject is an object.
"I have to mayry, I'm not up to two."
"All this makes me think of one thing, you,
at your age...think of it, it's the one big item
on your agenda----Do you really want
to live in the same room as anyone?"
                        *WITH*

[DOUBT]

[I. Draw]

2    the backs of the ~~new~~ cards are black ~~an acre of black cards~~; ~~and yet~~ *forced by*
~~luck~~ by

        ~~luck~~                                                    [*UNKNOWN HAND*]
     *a blank field of black cards; and yet by luck*                  [*FB*]


4    and lead the one card I had ~~promised~~ sworn to hold.


6–8  ~~by~~ but I remember the number on my card,
     a figure no philosopher takes to bed ,,, *[dots]*               [*FB*]
     Should revelations be held like private letters,


2. Pointing the Horn^s of the Dilemma

5    it is a room to walk' take notes, cross out .                  [*FB*]

8–14  "~~They~~ *We* just aren't up to your co^m ing home          [*FB*]
     three weeks, then leaving for three months. ~~They~~ *We* just aren't.  [*FB*]
     ~~They~~ *We* can't take much more of anything,                [*FB*]
     ~~they~~ *we* are so tired and hurt and worn. ~~They~~ *We* go on,  [*FB*]
     ~~know~~ knowing your real sickness is a ~~willful~~ *vacant*   [*FB*]
     deafness to little children . . . ~~I~~ and I suspect          [*FB*]
     it's impossible for anyone to help you."                       [*FB*]

                          ↖ *no italics*                            [*FB*]

DOUBT

I. Draw

The cardtable is black, the cards are played face down,
~~the backs of the cards are black; and yet by luck~~    *now*
I draw one card I wished to leave unchosen,
and lead the one card I had ~~promised~~ to hold.    *SWORN*
Dreams lose color faster than fair flowers,
~~by~~ I remember the number on my card,    *807*
a figure no philosopher takes to bed,,,    *L—[date]*
Should revelations be held like private letters,
till all the beneficiaries are dead,
and proper names become improper lives?
Focus about me and a blur inside,
on walks the things nearest me go slow motion,
obscene streetlife rushes on the wheelrim,
steel shavings from the vacillating will.

*a blank field of black cards; and yet by luck*

2. Pointing the Horn of the Dilemma

From the dismay of old marriage to the blanks
in another---water-torture of vacillation!
The true snakepit isn't monodrama Medea,
the gorgon arousing the serpents in her hair;
it is a room to walk, take notes, cross out
the notes, and gaze and walk and court diversion.
She loved me too much to have my welfare at heart:
"~~They~~ just aren't up to your coming home    *We*
three weeks, then leaving for three months. ~~They~~ just aren't.
~~They~~ can't take much more of anything,    *We*
~~they~~ are so tired and hurt and worn. ~~They~~ go on,    *We*
~~know~~ your real sickness is a ~~willful~~    *KNOWING*    *vacant*
deafness to little children...~~I~~ suspect ~~and~~ *I*
it's impossible for anyone to help you."

*└ no italics*

[(Doubt)]

[3. Critic]

3–5 ~~By what fireside shall I stretch my snakeskin~~
~~soiled by sliding and insinuation?~~
*Do you know how you have changed from the true you?*                    [*FB*]

*I would change my trueself if I could:*                    [*FB*]

I am do<sup>u</sup>btful . . . uncertain my big steps.


7–8 cutting ~~my brown~~ <sup>the blown</sup> rose from ~~its~~ <sup>my *the*</sup> still green thorns.  [*FB*]

My critic ma<sup>u</sup>st keep ~~a sharper~~ <sup>her sharpest</sup> tongue for praise.  [*FB*]


14 hoping for choice' the child of vacillation.                    [*FB*]

(Doubt)

3. Critic

My wickedness is not an honorable subject
for conversation---the flicker of the fading thing.
~~By what fireside shall I stretch my snakeskin~~
~~soiled by sliding and insinuation?~~
I am doubtful...uncertain my big steps.
I fear I leave a hole for the sharp knife
cutting ~~my brown~~ rose from ~~the~~ still green thorns. *THE BLOWN*
My critic m~~u~~st keep ~~a sharper~~ tongue for praise. *HER SHARPEST*
Only blood-donors retain a gift for words.
Blood brings sensation to everything that lives,
even to limbo where tried spirits sigh,
doing nothing the day because they think
imagination matures from doing nothing,
hoping for choice, the child of vacillation.

*Do you know how you have changed from the true you?*

*I would change my trueself if I could:*

~~LONDON AND~~ WINTER *AND LONDON*

[I. Closed Sky]                              *out*

7–9    ~~and~~ naked heaven's monologue with man.
       In ~~America, a wet~~ <sup>my country, the wettest</sup> Englishma<sup>e</sup>n
       sparkles with approbation, magnifying


out

~~2. Nineteenth Century Dutch Houses~~

4      grandfather, grandmother and maiden aunt ~~dis~~<sup>re</sup>placed

7–8    They cannot ~~catch~~ <sup>match</sup> us in the art of gutting.
       Angular houses tremble<sup>ing</sup> up six stories

11     high jungle-gyms of ~~predeluvian~~ <sup>aboriginal</sup> pipes. —

~~LONDON AND~~ WINTER *AND LONDON*

### I. Closed Sky

A hundred mornings meet the same closed sky,
one of nature's shows, one mantle wrapping
the dust of London with the dust of Europe---
in the interiors it is always night.
The clouds are welcome as a weather-break,
a silencer to the ultimate blue sky,
~~and~~ naked heaven's monologue with man.
In ~~America, a wet~~ Englishm~~an~~ *& MY COUNTRY, THE WETTEST*
sparkle~~s~~ with approbation, magnifying
curious small things we could never bear---
under closed sky, such things are luminous;
gossip makes New York and London one,
one tongue...both use identical instruments
for putting up a house and pulling down.

*out)*

~~(2)~~ Nineteenth Century Dutch Houses

One didn't like their houses when they stood;
soon the too solid oak was drawn and quartered,
knick-knacks dropped like spiders from the whatnot,
grandfather, grandmother and maiden aunt ~~dis~~placed *RE*
by bobbed couples of the swimming 'twenties,
to shallow to pull down the homes they left.
They cannot ~~catch~~ us in the art of gutting. *MATCH*
Angular houses tremble up six stories *ING*
to dissimilar Dutch and pie-slice-peaks,
held by the destroyer's scaffolding,
high jungle-gyms of ~~predeluvian~~ pipe~~s~~. *aBORIGINAL*
Last century Gothic brick has a sour redness
that time. I fear, does nothing to appease,
condemned by age, rebuilt by desolation.

(~~London and~~ Winter) *and ~~W~~ London)* [*FB*]

~~out~~ [*CB*]

[*FB*]

3. *2.* At <u>Offado's</u>

1      The Latin Quarter abuts on Be$^l$gravia

13–14  Leave me alone and let my$^e$ talk and love me—
       a cod in garlic, a carafe of cruel rosé. "    *[end quote]*   [*FB*]

~~out~~            ~~out ?~~ [*CB*]

[*FB*]

~~4.~~ *3.* ~~Flounder~~

2–5    to doomsday mornings. Crowds ~~herd~~ $^{crush}$ to work at eight,
       ~~lamp-white like couples leaving a midnight show.~~
       and walk with less cohesion than the mist;

       ~~The Thames is looped~~ at dawn $^{the\ Thames\ is\ still\ bright}$ with Christmas
            bulbs$;^,$
       $^{the\ sky}$ by nine A.M. is acid. God sees.

10–12  their ~~soles~~ $^{souls}$ are camouflaged to ~~lie~~ $^{die}$ in dishes, [*FB*]
       flat on their backs, the posture of forgiveness$;$--
       ~~elderberry$^,$ bloodshot, worldly eyes,~~
       double eyes bubbling bloodshot wor*ldli*ness, [*FB*]

14     at sea, the$^y$ bite like fleas whatever we toss.

(~~London and~~ Winter{and ~~to~~ London)

2. ~~3.~~ At <u>Offado's</u>

1

The Latin Quarter abuts on Begravia,
three floors low as one, blocks built of blocks,
insular eighteenth century laying down
the functional with a razor in its hand,
structures too practical for conservation.
An alien should count his change here, bring a friend.
Usually on weekend nights I eat alone;
you've taken the train for <u>Milgate</u> with the children.
At <u>Offado's</u>, the staff is half the guests,
the guitar and singers wait on table,
the artists sing things unconsolable:
"Girls of Majorca. Where is my Sombero?
Leave me alone and let my talk and love me---
a cod in garlic, a carafe of cruel rosé." // [end quote]

3. ~~4.~~ Flounder

Just yesterday we passed from the northern lights
to doomsday mornings. Crowds herd to work at eight,    CRUSH
~~lamp-white like couples leaving a midnight show.~~
~~The Thames is looped~~ at dawn with Christmas bulbs
by nine A.M. the sky is acid. God sees.    THE THAMES IS STILL BRIGHT
Wash me as white as the soles we ate last night,
acre of whiteness, back of Dover sand,
cooked and skinned and white---the heart appeased.    Die
Soles live in depth, see not, spend not...eat;    souls
their ~~soles~~ are camouflaged to lie in dishes,
flat on their backs, the posture of forgiveness~~,~~--
~~elderberry, bloodshot, worldly eyes,~~
unable ever to turn the other cheek---
at sea, the bite like fleas whatever we toss.

DOUBLE EYES BUBBLING BLOODSHOT
                              WORLDLINESS,

AND WALK WITH LESS COHESION THAN
                    THE MIST;

~~MORE LONDON WINTER~~ *(London and Winter)* *(Winter and London)*  [*FB*]
out

*out*  [*CB*]

~~1. Wolverine~~

1    What ~~were~~ <sup>was</sup> the lessons of the wolverine,


*stay*  [*CB*]

~~2.~~ <sup>5. 4.</sup> Mastodon  [*FB*]


9    the heavens were ~~very~~ short of hearing then.

MORE LONDON WINTER (Winter and London)
(London at Winter)

out

1. Wolverine
was
What were the lessons of the wolverine,
the Canada of Earnest Seton Thompson,
first snow in the schoolbook, first Cartesian blank?
At the edge of the rumpled sky, a too-red glow,
an upright iron rail, derrick or steeple,
trappers freighting on snowshoes through the snow,
track of the wolfpack whellsaw to the church---
no need for preachers to tell me wolves eat meat,
improve the terror of the first trapped wolf...
A wolverine, no critic of frontier justice,
learning the jaws meant him, was greatly tested,
and hesitated to chew off his foot---
the leisure given to gather fear and spirit,
our first undated leap in evolution.

2. Mastodon

stay

They splashed red on the Jews about to be killed,
then ploughed them back and forth in captured tanks;
the wood was stacked, the chainsaw went on buzzing.
In the best of worlds, the jailors follow the jailed.
In some final bog, the mastodon,
curled tusks raised like trumpets to the sky,
sunk to their hips and armpits in red mud,
splashed red for irreversible liquidation---
the heavens were very short of hearing then.
The price of freedom is choking down the facts:
gnashed tusk, bulk-bruised bulk and a red splash.
Good narrative is cutting out description;
nature sacrifices heightening
for the inevitable closing line.

(More ~~London~~ ~~and~~ Winter) *and London)* [FB]

3. 4 *5.* Freud [FB]

6–8 ~~He chose the angular cheerfulness of London,~~
~~a house to finish his~~ ~~Moses was and Egyptian;~~
*At home in England's rude formality,* [FB]

*he proved that Moses must have been Egyptian;* [FB]

~~H~~^h^e loathed neurotics for the harm they do.

12–13 was liquidated at Belsen. ~~Ð~~^S^hould we die, [FB]
living in places we ~~learn~~ ^have learned^ to live in,

4. ~~5.~~ *6.* Harriet's Doodle [FB]

5.4 3. Freud

Is it honorable for a Jew to die as a Jew?
Even the German officials encouraged Freud
to go to Paris where at least he was known;
but what does it matter to have a following,
if no one, not even the concierge, says <u>good day?</u>
~~He chose the angular cheerfulness of London,~~
~~a house to finish his Moses was an Egyptian;~~
He loathed neurotics for the harm they do.
What do we care for the great man of culture---
Freud's relations were liquidated at Belsen,
Moses Cohn who had nothing to offer culture
was liquidated at Belsen. Should we die,
living in places we ~~learn~~ to live in,    *HAVE LEARNED*
completing the only work we're trained to do?

6.5. 4. Harriet's Doodle

On this blank page no worse, not yet defiled
by inspiration running black in type,
I see her sepia donkey laugh at me,
Harriet's doodle, me in effigy,
my passport photo to America
that lifts the soul and irritates the eye---
<u>M. de Maupassant va s'animal^iser.</u>
Somberer exiles brought their causes here,
and children crying up and down the stairs;
Freud found his statue, older Jewish prophets
bit in until their teeth had turned to chalk,
found names in London and their last persona,
a body cast up lifeless on this shore...
Family, my family, why are we so far?

*At home in England's rude formality,*
*he proved that Moses must have been Egyptian;*

143

# [TRANSATLANTIC CALL]

14    She tell$^s$ me to stop, we mustn't lose your money."

TRANSATLANTIC CALL

"We can't swing New York on less than thirty thousand,,
the bright lights dragging like a ball and chain,
the Liberal ruined by the Liberal school.
This is the price of your manic flight to London---
that closed provincial metropolis was never
an asylum for the mercurial American mind...
They say fear of death is a child's remembrance
of the first desertion. Our daughter knows no love
that doesn't bind her with presents, letters, visits,
things outward and visible. I've closed my mind
so long, I want to keep it closed, perhaps---
I had too much faith in my power to will elevation;
if our house goes, a species is extinct....
She tell me to stop, we mustn't lose your money."

S

[EXORCISM]

[I.]

1    ~~As we love we are~~. Autumn hardens

9    <sup>*to*</sup> wait in the anteroom of apprehension,                    *[CB]*

12   ~~their~~ <sup>*two*</sup> souls cocooned in mystery from the mob.       *[CB]*

[2.]

7–9  Melodrama with her stiletto heels
     stamping bullit-~~holes~~ <sup>wounds</sup> in the parquet.
     ~~My~~ <sup>*The*</sup> ~~lines are exotic,~~ The ~~*the*~~ lines are spell-bound, but ~~my~~ <sup>the</sup> plot
     familiar:                                                                *[CB]*
     *The lines are spell-bound, but the plot familiar:*                      *[FB]*

11–12 ~~I~~ <sup>You</sup> can't carry ~~my~~ talent like a suitcase,
      or ever lose it—what I ~~am I~~ <sup>love</sup>, I am.

EXORCISM

I.

As we love we are. Autumn hardens
the hoarfrost of the morning, I grow less;
slowly the bridal fury shows her tooth,
parading in invisible link mail---
the slur from greenness to sterility,
fall in New England textile gray.
You point your finger: What you love you are.
I know what it is for a woman to be left,
To wait in the anteroom of apprehension,
waiting for the braggart bridegroom, Winter.
The witch is purring for the exorcist,
Two their souls cocooned in mystery from the mob.
Your woman dances for you child in arms,
she is dancing for you, Baby-Skull-Smile.


2.

Today, as if I were home in Boston, snow,
the pure witchery-bitchery of my first home;
my window whitens like a movie screen,
specked, aglow, excluding rival prospect---
I can throw what I want on this blank screen,
only the show I choose to show will show:
Melodrama with her stiletto heels
The stamping bullit-holes in the parquet.          WOUNDS THE
My lines are exotic, but my plot familiar.   THE LINES ARE SPELL-BOUND,
one man, two women, the common novel plot...             THE
You I can't carry my talent like a suitcase,
or ever lose it---what I love, I am.
Don't you dare mail us the love your life denies;
do you really know what you have done?


The lines are spell-bound, but the plot familiar:

147

[PLOTTED]                    ᵤ̶ᵤ̶ₜ̶

6     as I execute ~~my~~ ᵃ written plot.

PLOTTED

Planes arc like arrows through a higher sky,
ducks court in V's across the puckered pond;
Providence turns animals to things.
I roam from bookstore to bookstore browsing books,
I too maneuvered on a guiding string
as I execute my written plot.
I feel how Hamlet, stuck with the Revenge Play
his father wrote him, went scatological
under this beclotted London sky.
Catlike on a paper parapet,
he declaimed the words his prompter fed him,
knowing convention called him forth to murder,
loss of free will and licence of the stage.
Death's not an event in life, it's not lived through.

[THE COUPLE]

3–5     We were out walking. You ask, "What sort of street,
        London or shining?" "It was our own street."
        "Whatdid you do and hear?" "We heard ourselves;

8–12    happily, they ~~broke~~ failed ~~before we slipped.~~ *they melt before we slip.*     [*CB*]
        Our manner had some intimacy in ~~our~~ my dream."
        "What were you having out with such fair play?"
        "Our conversation held to a single plot,
        two women married to a ~~common task;~~ single man;

THE COUPLE

"Twice in the past two weeks I think I met
with Lizzie in the recurrent dream.
We were out walking. You ask, "What sort of street,
London or shining?" "It was our own street.
"Whatdid you do and hear?" "We heard ourselves;
the sidewalk was two feet wide. We, arm in arm,
squelching the five-point oakleaves under heel---
happily, they broke before we slipped.     *they melt before we slip.*   *failed*
Our manner had someintimacy in our dream.   *my*
"What were you having out with such fair play?"
"Our conversation held to a single plot,
two women married to a common task;   *SINGLE MAN;*
quotation dramatized the dialogue---
we were talking like sisters...you did not exist."

[ARTIST'S MODEL]

[1.]

3    Manet's bottles mirrored behind his bar-girl ~~are brigh~~

6    ~~My~~ <sup>Our</sup> children's children will have to ~~make~~ <sup>find</sup> their own;

10   I‸ haven't melted like a cube of sugar—

[2.]

4–11  ~~the naked departure of the artist's model~~
      ~~is cloaked~~ <sup>fogged</sup> ~~by her~~ ~~in her~~ *by her* ~~Anglo-Irish elevation;~~                    [CB]
      ~~W~~<sup>w</sup>~~hite rum is~~ <sup>is</sup> ~~undetectable from tears.~~                    [FB]
      ~~We're done, my clothes fly into your borrowed suitcase,~~
      ~~the good months are~~ <sup>days is</sup> ~~flown, and this~~ <sup>it</sup> ~~too goes~~
      ~~in my ragbag of private whim and illusion~~
      ~~dubiously flung~~ ⟨together⟩ ~~on~~
      ~~my single~~ ⟨self-dramatizing⟩ ~~character.~~

      *knowing how tomorrow's migraine will tell how drink*                    [FB]
      *heightened the brutal flow of elocution=* . . .                    [FB]
      *~~White rum is undetectable from tears~~* . . .                    [FB]
      *We're done, my clothes fly into your borrowed suitcase,*          *[over]*   [FB]

13–14  unalterable<sup>y</sup> divorced from choice by choice,
       I'<del>ve</del> <sup>'ve</sup> come on walking off-stage backwards.                    [FB]
                                        ~~where~~

ARTIST'S MODEL

I.

  Hölderlin's thing with autumn and swan-scene
behind was something beautiful, wasn't it?
Manet's bottles mirrored behind his bar-girl ####b##g#
are brighter than the stuff she used to serve---
the canvas should support the artist's model.
*Our.* My children's children will have to make their own; *FIND*
we squeezed the juice, their job to eat the skin,
we put God on his knees, and now he's praying....
When I sit in my bath, I wonder why
I haven't melted like a cube of sugar---
fiction should serve us with a slice of life;
but you and I actually lived what I have written,
the drunk-luck venture of our lives sufficed
to keep our profession solvent, was peanuts to live.


2.

  "If it were done, twere well it were done quickly---
to quote a bromide, your vacillation
is acne." We totter off the painter's platform, *ragged*
the naked departure of the artist's model
is cloaked by her Anglo-Irish elevation, *by her*
white rum is undetectable from tears. *is*
We're done, my clothes fly into your borrowed suitcase,
the good months are flown, and this too goes *Day is it*
in my ragbag of private whim and illusion
dubiously flung (together) on
my single (self-dramatizing) character.
Like a cat painfully backing down a tree,
unalterably divorced from choice by choice,
I come on walking off-stage backwards.

knowing how tomorrow's migraine will tell how
                                drink
heightened the brutal flow of elocution....
White rum is undetectable from tears...
We're done, my clothes fly into your borrowed
                              suitcase,

                              [over]

*the good day is flown, and it too goes*

*in a ragbag of private whim and illusion*

*dubiously borne by my single character.*

*~~Now no one backs down or loses an argument.~~*

*It would be redemptive not to have lived;*

*now no one backs down or loses an argument.*

[FB]

[FB]

[FB]

[FB]

[FB]

[FB]

*[then back to end of poem]*  [FB]

the good day is flown, and it too goes
in a ragbag of private whim and illusion
dubiously borne by my single character.

~~Now no one backs down or loses an argument.~~

It would be redemptive not to have lived;
now no one backs down or loses an argument.

[~~back~~ then to end of poem]

[(Artist's Model)]

[3.]

4–5    What I ~~am saying~~ <sup>*say*</sup> should go into your <u>Notebook:</u>    *[CB]*
I'd rather ~~have~~ my children on morphine than religion.

7    and you go on flapping in your ~~bed~~ <sup>*sheets*</sup>    *[CB]*

9–10    you will look for ~~my~~ <sup>the</sup> lof<sup>v</sup>e you fumble<sup>d</sup>, and see
only religion ~~caught~~ <sup>caught</sup> naked in the searchlights—

3.

"My mother really learned to loathe babies,
she loved to lick the palate of her Peke,
as if her tongue were trying a liqueur...
What I am saying should go into your Notebook:    say
I'd rather have my children on morphine than religion.
When you are dying, and your faith is sick,
and you go on flapping in your bed sheets
like a cockroach fallen in a fishbowl;
you will look for, and lose you fumble, and see   THE
only religion caught naked in the searchlights---   CAUGHT
Christians scream worse than atheists when they die.
What's so infamous about the death-ward
is they shove your bed nearer the door to move the corpse;
you know damn well it isn't for fresh air."

## [MERMAID EMERGING]

6      Law fit for all fits no one like a glove. ··

12–14  the only animal me$^a$n really love$^{s,}$ $^{**}$ $^s$

~~Mermaid or dolphin, you are fisherman's luck,~~
I spout the smarting waters of joy in your face."

r$^R$ough weather fist$^h,$ ~~that~~ $^{you}$ cuts our nets and chains.                                       ·

MERMAID EMERGING

The institutions of society
seldom look at a particular---
Degas's snubnosed dancer swings on high,
kicking the toplights, never leaving stage,
knowing lovers of art, discerning none.
Law fit for all fits no one like a glove...
Mermaid, why are you another species?
"Because, you, I, everyone is unique."
Does anyone ever make you do anything?
"Do this, do that, do nothing; you're not chained.
I am a woman and I am a dolphin,
the only animal men really love, *S
~~Mermaid or dolphin, you are fisherman's luck,~~
~~Rough weather fish that cuts our nets and chains.~~
→YOO
I SPOUT THE SMARTING WATERS OF JOY IN YOUR
FACE."

(Marriage?)

5. ¹· Angling

1    Withdrawn to a third your size, ~~and~~ ᵗʰᵒᵘᵍʰ frowning questions,

3    when ~~when~~ ᵗʰᵉ ʷⁱⁿᵉ takes liberty and loosens tongues—

9–10  your flights are covered by a laughing croak, ⎯
    ~~your~~ ª flowered dress ~~sinks~~ ˡᵒˢᵗ in a flowered wall.

12    the time to ~~sat~~ ᶜᵃˢᵗ is now, and the mouth open,


6. ²· Tired Iron

1    Mulch of the tired iron, stitch of the straffing planes—

3    still ~~once a~~ ⁱᵗ ʰᵃᵈ cleanness, now the smelly iron,

10–12 flesh of my body, one in our severalness.⎯
    ~~U~~ᵘnwilling to marry' ~~me,~~ ' ʸᵉᵗ ᵃⁿᵈ disloyal to woman
    in your airʸ willingness to submit,

*Marriage?*

1. 5. Angling

THOUGH

Withdrawn to a third your size, and frowning questions,
you sit silent through the afterdinner,   THE
when when takes liberty and loosens tongues--- WINE
fair-faced, ball-eyed, profile of a child,
except your eyelashes are always blacked,
each hair colored and quickened like tying a fly.
If words amuse you, the room includes your voice,
you are audible; none can catch you out,
your flights are covered by a laughing croak,--
a your flowered dress sinks in a flowered wall.  LOST
I am waiting like an angler with practice and courage;
the time to set is now, and the mouth open,  CAST
the huge smile, head and shoulders of the dolphin---
I am swallowed up alive...I am.

2. 6. Tired Iron

Mulch of tired iron, stitch of the straffing planes---
surely the great war of our youth was hollow;
still once a cleanness, now the smelly iron, ITHGO
the war on leaves, and the noyades of rice.
We promised to put back Liberty on her feet...
I can't go on with this, the measure is gone:
a waterfall, the water white on green,
like the white letters on my olive keyboard---
to stray with you and have you with me straying,
flesh of my body, one in our severalness--
Unwilling to marry, me, disloyal to woman, YET AND
in your air, willingness to submit,
preferring to have your body broken to being
unbreakable in this breaking life.

(Marriage?)

7. ³· Leaf-Lace Dress

3      it falls like bits of melting ~~iron or tin,~~ *tin on iron,*      [*FB*]

9      hag ~~summer~~ ^harvest^ has worn her ~~swollen~~ *swelling* shirt to dirt.      [*FB*]

13–14  I have walked five miles, ^and^ still desire to throw
       my feet off, be asleep and young . . . als*ʹ*eep.      [*CB*]


8. ⁴· Gruff

4–5    Weʼ ~~were~~ almost joined ^in marriage^ as our parents ~~were—~~
       short of disaster! ~~This~~ ^Love^ means giving the wheel

7      in the heel of my hand; ~~this~~ ^it^ means to turn

9      We might have married as Christ say^s^ man must not      [*FB*]

12–14  You ~~must not~~ ^cannot^ sell ~~this~~ ^our^ flight to ~~a~~ ma^e^n in bi^o^ndage·      [*FB*]
       ~~what's left if~~ ^with^ ~~marriage is outlaw~~^ed?~~ ~~"It could be heaven,~~
       ~~if such a thing is," you gruff into the phone.~~
       *When marriage is surmounted, what is left?*      [*FB*]
       *"Heaven, if such things are," you gruff into the phone.*      [*FB*]

(Marriage?)

3. 7. Leaf-Lace Dress

Leaf-lace, a simple intricate design---
if you were not inside it, nothing much; ~tin~
it falls like bits of melting ~iron or tin,~ (ON IRON,)
you fall perhaps metallic and as good.
Hard to work out the fact that makes you good,
whole spirit wrought from toys and nondescript,
though nothing less than the best woman in the world.
Cold the green shadows, iron the seldom sun,
hag summer has worn her ~swollen~ shirt to dirt.      HARVEST    swelling
Agony says we cannot live in one house,
or under my common name. This was the sentence---
I have lost everything . I feel a strength,
I have walked five miles, still desire to throw  AND
my feet off, be asleep and young...asleep.


4. 8. Gruff

The sky should be clearing, but it cannot lighten,
the unstable muck flies through the garden trees,
there's morning in my heart but not in things.
We ~were~ almost joined as our parents ~were~---  IN MARRIAGE
short of disaster! ~This~ means giving the wheel  LOVE
a shake that scatters spurs of displaced bone,
in the heel of my hand; ~this~ means to turn  IT
on my star hard, on my external star.
We might have married as Christ say man must not
in heaven where marriage is not, and giving
in marriage has the curse of God and Blake.
You ~must not~ sell ~this~ our flight to ~a~ men in bondage.
~what's left if marriage is outlaw~ ~"It could be heaven,~
~if such a thing is, you gruff into the phone.~

        CANNOT

When marriage is surmounted, what is left?
"Heaven, if such things are," you gruff into the phone.

[(Marriage?)]

*out*

9. ⁵· Marriage?

8      things will come out right with us, perhaps.

10     ~~made~~ ᵉᵃᶜʰᵉᵈ Yorkshire and ~~its~~ ᵗʰᵉ one-lane Roman roads,

(Marriage?)

5.♮. Marriage?

"I think of you every minute of the day,
I love you every minute of the day;
you gone is hollow, bored, unbearable.
I feel under some emotional anaesthetic,
unable to plan or think or write or feel;
maisacárira, these things will go, I feel
in an odd way against appearances,
things will come out right with us, perhaps.
As you say, we got across the Godstow Marsh,
made Yorkshire and its one-lane Roman roads,  THE
scaled Hadrian's Wall, and scared the stinking Pict.
Marriage? But that's another story. We saw
the diamond glare of morning on the tar.
For a minute had the road as if we owned it."

REACHED

~~LOST FISH~~ ~~SICKDAY~~ *LEAVING AMERICA FOR ENGLAND* [*FB*]

[I. Leaving America for England?]

1–5   ~~A~~ <sup>My</sup> lifelong taste for fishing the same waters—
<sup>a</sup> day is day there, America all landscape,
<sup>an</sup> ocean monolithic past weathering;
~~our sand is granite,~~ *~~the~~* our *coast drinks the ocean,* nature tends to gulp. ··
·                                                    [*FB*]

I held ~~back~~ <sup>to</sup> youth by rowing half a summer,

10   ~~A~~ <sup>Most</sup> survivor<sup>s</sup> ~~learns~~ to fall feet-first at birth.

12–14  <sup>through</sup> the ~~entertainment of~~ entertainment of uncertainty. <sup>of</sup>
        ~~entertainment and~~
·
        *through the entertainment of uncertainty.*         [*FB*]

Overtrained for England, ~~I~~ <sup>I</sup> find America ···
under unmoved heaven,changing sky.
                   ↖ *no comma*         [*FB*]

[2. Lost Fish]

1   ~~Beginning as a boy, I fished off-shore═~~
    A heavy step is weakest in the shallows—

5   roam<sup>ing</sup> down the shallows worn to bone.

10   drowned stumps, muskrat hut<sup>s</sup>, my record fish,

13   ~~remarried to our native elements.~~
    I reach the end of marriage on my knees.

~~POEM###~~ ~~SICKDAY~~ LEAVING AMERICA FOR ENGLAND

1. Leaving America for England?

MY
A lifelong taste for fishing the same waters---
an day is day there, America all landscape,
aN ocean monolithic past weathering;
~~our sand is granite~~, nature tends to gulp.... *the coast drinks the ocean,*
*70*
I held ~~back~~ youth by rowing half a summer,
but aging becomes a habit: puzzles repeated
and remembered, games repeated and remembered,
the runner trimming on his mud-smooth path,
the gamefish fattened in its narrow channel.
A survivor learns to fall feet-first at birth. MOST
Help me from seeing through anyone I love,
the entertainment of uncertainty. *through the entertainment*
Overtrained for England, I find America,-- *of uncertainty.*
under unmoved heaven changing sky.
THROUSI              no comma

2. Lost Fish

~~Beginning~~ as a boy, I fished off-shore--
once squinting in the sugared eelgrass for game,
I saw the glass torpedo of a big fish,
power strayed from unilluminating depth,
iNG roam down the shallows worn to bone.
I was seven, and fished without a hook---
luckily, Mother was still omnipotent....
A battered sky, a more denuded lake,
my heavy rapier trolling rod bent L,
drowned stumps, muskrat hut, my record fish,
its endless waddling outpull like a turtle;
then my line snaps, or the knot pulls; we are loose,
~~remarried to our native elements~~.
The mud we stirred sinks in the lap of plenty.

A HEAVY STEP IS WEGHEST IN THE SHALLOWS

I REACH THE END OF MARRIAGE ON MY KNEES.

~~(Sickday)~~ *(Leaving America for England)*

[3. Sickday]

4–5 ~~I face my false condition~~ ^confession^ ~~and true life.~~
*If by illness I might find perspective....*

On this sickday, I ‸earn the beautiful:

7 saloons for ~~Irish poets~~ ^monologue and^ Irish poets,

(~~Sickday~~) (leaving America for England)

3. Sickday

The four P.M. orange and black sky,
the sun struggling to renounce ascendency---
two elephants are hauling at my head.
> ~~I face my false condition and true life.~~    CONFESSION
On this sickday, I learn the beautiful:
a castle, ducks, old polished heirloom servants,
saloons for monologue and Irish poets,
Alka Seltzer on each bedside table,
fish for the table bunching in the fishpond.
None of us can or wants to tell the truth,
or underplay the fish we lost, while floating
the lonely river to senility.
It's an open ending. Sometimes in sickness,
love is simple enough to enter heaven.

> If by illness I might find perspective....

~~Marriage?~~

⌐BEFORE WOMAN⌐?? ?                    *question mark*

[I. Before the Dawn of Woman]

8–10    You‸hold me in the hollow of your hand—
          a man is free to play, and then he ~~slackens;~~<sup>s;</sup>
          ~~he is~~ shifty past the reach of ridicule.

14      like the animals, I am humorless."

[2. Dawn]

3–4    our ancestors declared all men are evil;      *[semi-colon]*
      ~~but~~ no one who can live is wholly damned.

8      My springless step still stalks ~~the~~ <sup>for the</sup> youngman's wildweed,

10     the goldfinch-nest defying ~~all~~ euphemism.

12–13 Darling, the cork, though fat and black, still pulsls,
       and new wine floods ~~our~~ <sup>the our</sup> prehistoric veins<sup>s</sup>—

BEFORE WOMAN ? ← question mark

I. Before the Dawn of Woman

"Gazing close-up at your underjaw,
a blazon of barbaric decoration,
a sprinkle of black rubies, clots from shaving,
panting in measure to your wearied breath,
I see the world before the dawn of woman,
the jungle of diehard males, their scab of rapine,
rhinocerus on Eden's rhinocerus rock...
Youhold me in the hollow of your hand---
a man is free to play, and then he slackens,
he is shiftybpast the reach of ridicule.
A woman loving is serious and disarmed,
she is less distracted than a pastured mare,
munching as if life depended on munching...
like the animals, I am humorless."


2. Dawn

Even a parrot-man can write good books,
live out his second-rate, most writers do;    [semi-colon]
our ancestors declared all men are evil,
but no one who can live is wholly damned.
Living with you is living a long book,
War and Peace, from day to day to day,
unable to look off or hear my name.  FOR THE
My springless step still stalks the youngman's wildweed,
the God-borne instant never letting up,
the goldfinch-nest defying all euphemism.
Where will you take me in the fizz of winter?
Darling, the cork, though fat and black, still pulls,
and new wine floods our prehistoric veins---
the day breaks, impossible, in our bed.

THE
OOR

[FLIGHT TO NEW YORK]

[I. Fox-Fur]

6–7   knob rising in the grizzled fox-fur collar...'
      <sup>But</sup> I~~n~~ fear rejection and will stall . . .

10–11  in the last ~~wto~~ *two* months, she's stopped being a child,
      she's a friend to <u>Mom</u> now, not an enemy,        *[FB]*

13    She says ~~that~~ God is only ~~a~~ *another* great man,        *[FB]*


[2. <u>The Messiah</u>]

1     "I love you so' Darling, there's a black void,        *[FB]*

7     and ~~drink~~ <sup>eat</sup> at the <u>Russian Tearoom</u> afterward?

10    I wait for your letters' tremble when I get none,        *[FB]*

FLIGHT TO NEW YORK


I. Fox-Fur

"I have recruited the services of good
old <u>Farrar, Straus and Giroux</u>, and even if
the taxi strike is off, their limousine is ours.
I met Ivan in a marvelous fox-fur coat,
his luxurious squalor...and gave you one...your grizzled
knob rising in the grizzled fox-fur collar~~~~~~~;
*But* In fear rejection and will stall...
You're not under inspection, just missed;
and you'll be pleased with Harriet:
in the last ~~two~~ months, she's stopped being a child,
she's a friend to <u>Mom</u> now, not an enemy,
except for my yelling, <u>Dammit, brush your teeth.</u>
She says ~~that~~ God is only a great man,  *another*
a ape with grizzled sideburns in a cage."


2. <u>The Messiah</u>

"I love you so, Darling, there's black void,
as black as night without you. I long to see
your face and hear your voice and take your hand,
laugh with you, gossip and catch up...or down.
Will you go with me to The Messiah,
on December 17th, a Thursday,
and drink at the <u>Russian Tearoom</u> afterward?   *cut*
I am going out for the tickets this morning,
your dear, longed-for presence going with me.
I wait for your letters, tremble when I get none,
more when I do. Nothing new to say;
I've not been feeling too well; it will have passed
by the time this letter arrives---just cold and nausea;
when I mail this and get <u>The Messiah</u> tickets, I'll rest."

## [FLIGHT TO NEW YORK]

1. ~~1.~~ ~~2.~~ 3. Plane-Ticket
2      more than ever flying seems to° lofty,

5      The London damp comes in, its smell so keen

7      in the ~~damp of~~ <sup>ass same damp as</sup> thirty-five years ago in Nashville,

9–10   y<sup>t</sup>wenty-five years of marriage, a book of life,
        <sup>with</sup> two endings. I have bought my round-trip ticket . . .

13      ~~the~~ shellac and crassness of a new suit, a feeling,

2. ~~2.~~ 3 4. *~~Departur~~ ~~Par~~ Departure* At the Air-Terminal             *[FB]*

10      I know I am happier <sup>with</sup> ~~I~~ <sup>you</sup> than before;

12      My signal flashes. ~~My~~ <sup>The</sup> plane is at the door.

FLIGHT TO NEW YORK

**3.**
1. 1. Plane-Ticket

A virus and its hash of knobby aches---
more than ever flying seems to lofty,
the weather unlucky for visiting New York,
for telephoning kisses transatlantic...
The London damp comes in, its smell so keen
trees grow in my room. I'm reading Ford's <u>Some Do Not</u>,
in the damp thirty-five years ago in Nashville,   *some damps*
same book. What changes only changes a fraction---
*t* twenty-five years of marriage, a book of life,
*with* two endings. I have bought my round-trip ticket...
After fifty so much joy has come,
I can hardly clothe the seams of my body---
the shellac and crassness of a new suit, a feeling,
not wholly happy, of having been reborn.

**4.** Departure *Departure*
2. 2. At the Air-Terminal

London a Chinese gray or oyster gray,
every apalling shade of pitch-pitch gray---
no need to cook up far-fetched imagery
to establish a climate for our mood---
anything's real until it's published.
"If I have had hysterical drunken seizures,
it's from loving you too much. It makes me wild,
I fear. I'll make the dining-room a bedroom.
I feel unsafe, uncertain you'll come back.
I know I am happier with you than before;
my pains were always girdled about with joy."
My signal flashes. My plane is at the door.  *The*
Our gold rings touch. Surely, it was great joy
blaming ourselves and wanting to do wrong.

*1*

[(Flight to New York)]

~~3.~~ ⁴⁵. Flight

2–3    I ~~bear~~ ᵇʳⁱⁿᵍ my body, almost my best friend,
       my amanuensis at home ₐ ~~for weeks~~ ᵃˡˡ ᵈᵃʸ

6    ~~I live.~~ *[beginning of line]* ~~I manage, born~~ A generation later, ~~I might~~    *[FB]*
        ~~I could~~ I could *[end of line]*    *[FB]*
       *~~I manage,~~ Born a generation later, I could*    *[FB]*


~~4.~~ ⁵ ⁶. New York Again

1    After ~~l~~ᴸondon, the wind, the eye, my thoughts

4    no queuᵉs for busses and every angle right,    *[FB]*

9    a love of features fame ~~has~~ putˢ ~~on~~ ᵘᵖ ~~for~~ ⁽ˢᵗᵉᵗ⁾ sale—

5.4 7. Flight

I am better company if depressed...
I bear my body, almost my best friend, *BRING*
my amanuensis at home ~~for weeks~~ *act Day*
typing out worksheets for the gulping guest.
If I cannot love myself, can you?
~~I live A~~ generation later, ~~I might~~ *I manage, BORN*
have learned to cook and feed the baby--- ~~I could~~
no plum. I am your friend from out of town,
in flight to New York....I see the rising prospect,
the scaffold glitters, the concrete walls are white,
flying like Feininger's skyscraper yachts,
geometrical romance in the river mouth,
conical foolscap dancing in the sky...
the runway growing wintry and distinct.

*I could F [end?]*

6.8 4. New York Again      ~~Frances~~, *Born a generation later, I could*

After London, the wind, the eye, my thoughts
race through New York with gaping coarse-comb teeth,
the simple-minded streets are all one-way,
no queus for busses and every angle right,
a huddled London with twenty times the soaring;
it is fish-shaped, it is modern, it is metal,
austerity assauged with melodrama,
an irritable reaching after fact and reason,
a love of features fame has put on sale--- *up for (stop)*
love is all here, and the house desolate.
What shall I do with my stormy life blown towards evening?
No fervor helps without the favor of heaven,
no permissive law of nature pays the bill---
survival is talking on the phone.

*[beginning of line]*

[(Flight to New York)]

7. ^6. 7. No Messiah

4–5    ◄—Even ~~in~~ the licence of my mind, ^rebels,
        ~~I find~~ ^and has no empty room for ~~our~~ ^my two lives.

9      ~~Still~~ ^Planesick on New York food, I feel the old subway

8. ^7. 8. Sleepless

9      that hold^s, and never fumbles the transcendence

11     All my friends are writers. ^Do ~~W~~^We deserve

13–14  self-seeking with a persistent tenderness
        rivals seldom lavish on a brother.^?

(Flight to New York)

7.

## 7. No Messiah

Sometime I must try to write the truth,
but almost everything has fallen awry
in the eight months since we said goodbye in Rome.
Even in the licence of my mind, *REBELS,*
I find no empty room for our two lives. *My AND HGS*
Some things like death are meant to have no outcome.
I come like someone naked in my raincoat,
but only a girl is naked in a raincoat.
Still planesick on New York food, I feel the old subway
reverberating in our apartment floor,
I stop in our Christmas-streamered bedroom, hearing
my Nolo, the non-Messianic man---
drop, drop in silence, then a louder drop
echoed elsewhere by a louder drop.

8.

## 8. Sleepless

Home for the night on my last ten years' workbed,
where I asked the facing brick for words, and woke,
a haggard mask of imbecility,
hearing then as now the distant, panting siren,
small as a harbor boat patrolling the Hudson,
persistent cry without diminishment
or crescendo through the sleepless hours.
I hear its bland monotony, the voice
that holds and never fumbles the transcendence
I fiddled for imperiously and too long.
All my friends are writers. We deserve *Do*
to sleep, because we gave our selves the breaks,
self-seeking with persistent tenderness
rivals seldom lavish on a brother.

[(Flight to New York)]

7 ⁹. Christmas 1970

4  whole truth—one ~~is~~ true as another: "I cannot tell you

8–9 we have no choice." It's true, w<sup>W</sup>e . . . . ~~We?~~ <u>We</u> · · · <u>we?</u> Things pass.
   Our Christmas tree ~~has~~ <sup>seems</sup> fallen out with nature,

11  At ~~best~~ <sup>worst</sup> the time is not unhappy, green sap

14  I waver<sup>ed</sup>, am counted with the living.

~~8.~~ ¹⁰· Christmas 1970

5  projector, a ~~thick~~ <sup>heavy</sup> book, sunrise-red from Lizzie,

8  Birdlike spirits<sup>s</sup>, slight burdens, no grave duty    *[FB]*

(Flight to New York)


9. Christmas 1970

All too often lately your voice is bright,
the voice of conscience verbal...I always hear you
waking me to myself: half-truth, untruth,
whole truth---one *is* true as another:"I cannot tell you
the things we planned for you this Christmas season.
I've written my family not to phone today;
we had to put away your photographs--- _____ *WE...WE?*
we have no choice." It's true. We....We? Things pass.
Our Christmas tree has fallen out with nature, *SEEMS*
shedding to a naked cone of triggered wiring.
At best the time is not unhappy, green sap *WORST*
still floods the arid rind, the thick boughs catch
the drafts, as if alive---I too, because
I waver, am counted with the living.
*ED*

10. 8. Christmas 1970

The tedium and deja-vu of home
make me love it; bluer days will come
and acclimatize the Christmas gifts:
redwood bear, rubber-egg shampoo, home-movie-
projector, a thick book, sunrise-red from Lizzie, *HEAVY*
with, "Why don't you try to lose yourself
and write a play about the fall of Japan?"
Birdlike spirits, slight burdens, no grave duty
to seem universally sociable
and polite...We are at home and warm,
as if we had escaped the gaping jaws---
underneath us like a submarine,
nuclear and protective like a mother,
swims the true shark, the shadow of departure.

# ~~THE~~ BURDEN  *~~too aroused I am afraid~~*  [CB]

## I. Knowing

2–7  I think of Grandfather and his poor last ~~nights~~ <sup>days</sup>
bringing his <u>tortures of the damned</u> to breakfast. *too aroused he was* *afraid*  [CB]

stet)  Caroline, he knew such naked ~~hours,~~ nights,
outliving ~~his~~ son, place, ~~and~~ fortune . . . their survivor
with nothing to will. Have we got a child? · · ·
Ө⁰ur bastard, easily fathered, hard to name?  [FB]

10–11  firm in the power of your impaʼtial heat.  [FB]
I'm not mad and hold to you with reason;ʼ

## [2. Three]

<u>out</u>  [CB]

2  Peéguy thought God the Father was a Frenchman;

4  ours <sup>child</sup> is a river, one without a surname,

8  Too much transcendence fades to symbols;

10–11  God help us three, and give us ~~on~~ that day . . .
Nothing ~~in~~ <sup>of</sup> us reflowers, except our childhood,

*toward damaged*

**▨ BURDEN**

**I. Knowing**

This night, tonight, I will not play or sleep,
I think of Grandfather and his poor last nights *Days*
bringing his tortures of the damned to breakfast. — *toward to memaford*
*57c1)* Caroline, he knew such naked hours, *NIGHTS*
outliving his son, place, and fortune...their survivor
with nothing to will. Have we got a child?..
Our bastard, easily fathered, hard to name?
Illegible, bracketted with us? My hands
sleep on the bosom of your sleeping hand,
firm in the power of your impatial heat.
I'm not mad and hold to you with reason,
you carry our burden to the narrow strait,
this sleepless night that will not move, yet moves
unless by sleeping we think back yesterday.

**2. Three**

All is not dead, but everything feels dying;  *← cut*
Péguy thought God the Father was a Frenchman;
God couldn't father children without our lapse---
ours/is a river, one without a surname,  *RCHICO*
promise unconvertible to water,
formless, a rush of black and scarlet brush-sweep...
Look deep as we will, we cannot see our likeness.
Too much transcendence fades to symbol;
our child is someone, the someone we will meet.
God help us three, and give us on that day...
Nothing in us reflowers, except our childhood,  *OF*
death is less of a leap than getting born.
Every writer, every journeyman,
past the halfway, is Keats at twenty-four.

[(The Burden)]

3. ² ~~The~~ Question  [*FB*]

4      and answers the question ˢ. Fifteen years ago,

9–11    a poor game for ᵃ ~~fathers~~ when I ~~was young,~~ ᵃᵐ ᵒⁿᵉ,
        nature a wild card in the numbered ~~deck~~ ᵖᵃᶜᵏ . . .
        In body, I still seem ~~a buck~~ ᵗᵒ ʷⁱⁿ up here,

4. ³ Overhanging Cloud  [*FB*]

7–9      ~~These d~~ᴰull clouds often ᶜʰᵃⁿᵍᵉ ᵗᵒ dazzle in a minute;
        we do not grow with our children in the ~~the~~ womb,
        ~~have visions~~ ˢᵉᵉ ˢᵃᵗᵃⁿ like Milton going blind in London,

11–13    and ~~face~~ ˢᵉᵉ the needle-fire of the first light
        bombarding ~~on~~ ᵒᶠᶠ your ~~young~~ eyelids harmlessly.
        ~~Clouds are rain and fertile~~ ~~mothers.~~*maternal* . And now the room is sultry.
           You double-breathe,  [*CB*]

2. 3. The Question

> I ask doggishly into your face---
> dogs live on guesswork, heavens of submission,
> but only the future lies in true touch,
> and answers the question: Fifteen years ago,
> Harriet was this burdensome questionmark.
> I fish up my old words, <u>Dear</u> and <u>Dear Ones.</u>
> Will the lucky number I threw down
> come twice? Living is not a numbers game,
> a poor game for fathers when I was young,
> nature a wild card in the numbered deck...
> In body, I still seem a buck up here,
> I eat, drink, sleep and put on clothes up here,
> I'll get my books back when we've lived together---
> in this room on which all other rocks bear down.

3 4. Overhanging Cloud

> This morning the overhanging cloud is piecrust,
> a Temple of Luxor based on rich runny ooze;
> my old life settles down into the archives.
> It's strange having a child today, though common,
> adding our further complication to
> intense fragility.
> Those Dull clouds often dazzle in a minute;
> we do not grow with our children in the womb,
> have visions, like Milton going blind in London,
> but it's enough to wake without old fears,
> and face the needle-fire of the first light
> bombarding on your young eyelids harmlessly.
> Clouds are rain and fertile. You double-breathe,
> we are many, our bed smells of hay.

[(The Burden)]

5. ⁴ Gold Lull  [FB]

2–9     as naturally, the belly of ~~my~~ <sup>the</sup> breeding
      ~~lover is swell's ing~~ <sup>mother lifts</sup> to every breath ~~of~~ <sup>in</sup> sleep—
      Rubens's nudes needed no anaesthetic at childbirth.
      In this gold lull of sleep, ~~the~~ <sup>a</sup> muzzled ~~mother~~ <sup>lovers</sup>  [FB]
      lies<sup>s lies</sup> open and takes<sup>s takes</sup> the world for what it is,  [FB]
      a minute ~~less~~ <sup>more</sup> than a minute . . . as many a writer
      suffers<sup>eds</sup> illusions that his phrase might live:
      P<sup>P</sup>ower makes nothing happen, ~~deeds are words.~~ <sup>*words are deeds.*</sup>  [FB]


6. ⁵ Green Sore  [FB]

1     ~~The~~ too early squeaking country birds fatigue,

3–4    war of words, lung͵ of infinitude . . .
      The ~~postman~~ brings ~~America~~ to Kent:
      The morning mail brings the familiar voice to Kent:
      *The morning mail brings the familiar voice to Kent:*  [FB]


6–8    ~~The new spring fields extend~~ <sup>expose their trick</sup> ~~like a~~ <sup>are like a new</sup> ~~green~~
~~sore.~~
      ~~It~~ This *was* ~~our~~ the *green life, even heard through tears . . . .*  [FB]

      ~~We~~ <sup>We've</sup> pack<sup>ed</sup> ~~and'~~ leave <u>Milgate</u>, in a rush as usual
      for the ~~train to London~~ <sup>London train</sup>, leaving five lights burning—

(The Burden)

4 5. Gold Lull

This isn't the final calm...as easily,
as naturally, the belly of ~~my~~ breeding *THE MOTHER LIFTS*
~~lover in swelling~~ to every breath ~~of~~ sleep--- *IN*
Rubens'~~s~~ nudes needed no anaesthetic at childbirth.
In this gold lull of sleep, ~~the~~ muzzled ~~mother~~ *< CVCK#*
lie~~s~~/~~s~~open and take~~s~~ the world for what it is, *lies takes*
a minute ~~less~~ than a minute...as many a writer *MORE*
S  suffer~~s~~ illusions that his phrase might live:
~~power makes nothing happen, deeds are words.~~ *words are deeds.*
President Lincoln almost found this faith;
once a good ear could almost hear the heart
murmur in the square thick hide of Lenin....
If only successful statesmen had a chance,
courage to be merciful to the young.

5 6. Green Sore

~~The~~ too early squeaking country birds fatigue, *THE MORNING MAIL*
uxorious rattling of the pinhead rooks, *BRINGS THE FAMILIAR*
war of words, lung of infinitude... *VOICE TO KENT* *and like a*
The ~~postman~~ brings Ameri~~c~~a to Kent: *their*
"not that I wish you entirely well, far from it." *cheese X next*
~~The new spring fields extend like a green sore.~~ *NEW*
*Wait* ~~We~~ pack ~~and~~ leave Milgate, in a rush as usual
for the ~~train) to~~ London, leaving five lights burning---
to fool the burglar? Never the same five lights.
Sun never sets without our losing something:
books, keys, letters, or "Dear Caroline,
I have told Harriet that you are having a baby
by her father. She knows she will seldom see him;
physical presence or absence is the thing."

*THIS*
2) ~~It~~ was *the* ~~one~~ green life, even heard through tears....

1) The morning mail brings the familiar voice to Kent:

[(The Burden)]

[6. "I despair of letters . . ."]

2      interestested in the thing happening to you now.

(The Burden)


6. "I despair of letters..."

"I despair of letters. You say I wrote H. isn't
interested in the thing happening to you now.
So what? A fantastic untruth, misprint, something;
I meant the London scene's no big concern, just you...
She's absolutely beautiful, gay, etc.
I've a horror of turmoiling her before she flies
to Mexico, alone and brave, half-Spanish.
Children her age don't sit about talking out
the thing about their parents. I do talk about you,
and I have never denied I miss you...
I guess we'll make Washington this weekend;
it's a demonstration, like all demonstrations,
repetitious, gratuitous, unfresh...just needed.
I hope nothing is mis-said in this letter."

[(The Burden)]

[7. Later Week at <u>Milgate</u>]

3–4    the sun in heavens ~~warms~~ <sup>shines on</sup> *warms* a sanded floor.    *[FB]*

        For <sup>a</sup> moments. Age is ~~our~~ <sup>*our*</sup> resumption of dullness,    *[FB]*

6–9    no paint or skill with the knife ~~will~~ save<sup>s</sup> our finish.

        I still ~~think up~~ <sup>remember</sup> more things than I forget:

        once it was the equivalent ~~of~~ <sup>to</sup> everlasting

        to stay loyal to ~~the~~ <sup>my</sup> other person loved,

11–13  ~~I sit with my fresh wife, children, house and sky~~

        In the greenest apple lurks a breath of spirits—

        *In the greenest apple lurks a breath of spirits—*    *[FB]*

        I sit with my fresh wife, children, house and sky;‾

        ~~the sky's~~ <sup>heaven</sup> a smudge of mushroom. Here with luck,

[8. Nine Months]

1    For weeks' now, months, ~~this~~ <sup>the</sup> ~~Juno~~ <sup>burdened</sup> - year has ~~gone,~~

        ~~ripened,~~ gone

5    watching my nose bleed ~~scarlet-gloss~~ <sup>red lacquer</sup> on the grass;

11–14  ~~forgiving by forgetting. We're nine-tenths liquid,~~

        even ~~the sober~~ *abstainers* are nine-tenths liquid blood.    *[FB]*

        I see, smell, taste ~~the~~ <sup>our</sup> blood in everything.

        You move on crutches, ~~ninth month into tenth—~~ <sup>8th month into 9th,—</sup>

                               *[dash]*

                                *FB]*

        love in ~~the~~ fullness ~~of~~ of flesh and heart and humor.

(The Burden)

### 7. Later Week at <u>Milgate</u>

A sweetish smell of shavings, wax and oil
follows the redone room made young by antiquing;
the sun in heavens warms a sanded floor.
For a moment. Age is a resumption of dullness,
my varnish complaining: I will die forever;
no paint or skill with the knife will save our finish.
I still think up more things than I forget:
once it was the equivalent of everlasting
to stay loyal to the other person loved,
in Maine each rock a skull, our common gravestone....
In the greenest apple lurks a breath of spirits—
I sit with my fresh wife, children, house and sky;
the sky's a smudge of mushroom. Here with luck,
green grass till New Year---I, my wife, our children.

### 8. Nine Months

For weeks, now, months, this Juno-year has gone,
a happiness so slow burning, it is lasting.
The animated nettles are black slash.
September. Today I leaned too much on my elbows,
watching my nose bleed scarlet-gloss on the grass;
I can almost call our holding ours.
In a year you've leapt from 38 to 40,
joined the bench of women who can judge:
<u>woman has never forgiven man her blood.</u>
That indictment withers in your forgetfulness;
forgiving by forgetting. We're nine-tenths liquid,
I see, smell, taste the blood in everything.
You move on crutches, ninth month into tenth---
love in the fullness of flesh and heart and humor.

[(The Burden)]

[9. Morning Away from You]

1–2   A single swaying skeleton of black rose ~~leaves~~ <sup>tendril</sup>
metalled to my window, ⁻ oyster-gray

7–8   <u>Goodmorning.</u> My nose runs, ~~and~~ <sup>and</sup> I look for blood. ··
It's ~~strange~~ <sup>happy</sup> to find love with you at last,

11   like Mother and Father, <sup>their</sup> youths struck <sup>dead</sup> at sixty;

13–14  ~~When~~ I draw the curtain, ⁚ the sky's ~~blue=pale,~~ <sup>sky-blue.</sup>
the black rose-leaves ~~are~~ <sup>were</sup> <sup>are</sup> green—a good ∧ morning, as often. ⁚
[lines below]                                     [FB]

*I draw the curtain: a good morning, as often . . .*
*the sky's sky-blue, the black rose-leaves are green.*


[10. Robert Sheridan]

2–3   of ~~the child~~ <sup>(stet)</sup> ~~baby~~ the child , feet-first, ⁻ ~~a crumb~~ <sup>a string</sup> of tobacco
tied
to your throat that won't go down ~~. . .~~ ⁻ your window piled

5–7   ~~your~~ <sup>a the</sup> dinner like Kleenex— ···· t<sup>T</sup>oo much blood ~~is spilt,~~ <sup>seeped</sup>
                                 [?] *has*

        ~~seeped~~ ~~seeps off~~ is seeped*ing*—                    [CB]
        *of the child, feet-first, a string of tobacco tied*        [FB]
        *to your throat that won't go down —your window piled*    [FB]
        ~~with~~ *with brown bags leaking peaches and avocadoes . . .*   [FB]
        *dinner like Kleenex. . . . Too much blood is seeping—*    [FB]

   after <sup>the</sup> twelve hours labor to come out right, ·
~~in~~ <sup>with</sup> less than thirty seconds swimming ~~the~~ <sup>the</sup> flood-blood:

14   we have escaped our death-~~struggle~~<sup>fight</sup> with our lives."

9. Morning Away from You

*tenerife*

A single swaying skeleton of black rose leaves
metalled to my window, oyster-gray
Colchester, Hokusai's assertion of dearth;
it wrings a cry from me. My host's date,
apparently naked, carrying all her clothes
sways through the dawn in my bedroom to the shower.
Goodmorning. My nose runs, and I look for blood... *and*
It's strange to find love with you at last, *happy*
now death has become an ingredient of my being:
bloodclot and hemorage, today, tomorrow,
like Mother and Father, youth struck at sixty; *dead*
I have saved their blood, and hand it on....
When I draw the curtain, the sky's blue-pale, *sky-blue,*
the black rose-leaves are green---a goodmorning, as often:

*[line below]*    *were*    *than*
*are*

10. Robert Sheridan

*(stet)* Your midnight ambulances, the first knife-saw
of the child, feet-first, a crumb of tobacco tied *a string*
to your throat that won't go down...your window piled
with brown bags leaking peaches and avocados... *is seen*
your dinner like Kleenex-...too much blood *is seen*
after twelve hours labor to come out right,     ....
in less than thirty seconds swimming the flood-blood: *the*
Little Gingersnap Man, homoform,
contracted, flat and alcoholics' red,
only like us in owning to middle-age.
"If I touch him, I might burn my fingers."
"It's his health, not heat. Why are other babies pallid?
His navy-blue eyes tip with his head....Darling,
we have escaped our death-struggle with our lives."
*F 1917*


*I draw the curtain: a good morning, as often...*
*the sky's sky-blue, the black rose-leaves are green.*

*lines 2 - 5    of "Robert Sheridan":*
*of the child, feet-first, a string of tobacco tied*
*to your throat that won't go down — your window piled*
*with brown bags leaking peaches and avocados...*
*dinner like Kleenex.... Too much blood is sleeping —*

[DOLPHIN]

9  and plotted perhaps too fr̶eely *freely* with my life,  *[FB]*

12  yet ask̶i̶n̶g *ask* compassion for this book, half fiction,  *[FB]*

DOLPHIN

My Dolphin, you only guide me by surprise,
as helpless as Racine, the man of craft,
drawn through a maze or iron composition
by the incomparable wandering voice of Phedre.
When my mind was troubled, you made for my body
caught in its hangman knot of sinking lines,
a vitreous bowing and scraping of the will.
I have listened to too many words,
and plotted perhaps too freely with my life,    *freely*
not avoiding injury to person,
not avoiding injury to myself;
yet ask compassion for this book, half fiction,    *ask*
an eelnet made by man for the eel fighting.
Why should shark be eaten when the bait swim free?